TO THE LAST MAN

TO THE
LAST
MAN

A STORY
OF COURAGE
AND LOYALTY

GLEN ROBINSON

Pacific Press®
Publishing Association
Nampa, Idaho | www.pacificpress.com

Cover design by Steve Lanto
Cover design resources from iStockphoto.com/480462498
Inside design by Kristin Hansen-Mellish

Scripture quotations marked KJV are from the King James Version.

Scripture quotations marked NIV® are from THE HOLY BIBLE, NEW INTERNATIONAL VERSION®. Copyright © 1973, 1978, 1984, 2011 by Biblica, Inc.® Used by permission. All rights reserved worldwide.

The author assumes full responsibility for the accuracy of all facts and quotations as cited in this book.

Additional copies of this book may be purchased by calling toll-free 1-800-765-6955 or by visiting AdventistBookCenter.com.

Library of Congress Cataloging-in-Publication Data
Names: Robinson, Glen, 1953- author.
Title: To the last man : a story of courage and loyalty / Glen Robinson.
Description: Nampa : Pacific Press Publishing Association, 2018.
Identifiers: LCCN 2018018300 | ISBN 9780816364015 (pbk. : alk. paper)
Subjects: LCSH: Jonathan (Biblical figure)
Classification: LCC BS580.J57 R63 2018 | DDC 222/.4092—dc23 LC record available at https://lccn.loc.gov/2018018300

August 2018

Dedication

For Gavin.
May you find adventure in every step of your walk with God.

Contents

Contents

Preface

I t's been my intention for quite a while to write this story about Jonathan. It's a story filled with intrigue, heroism, excitement, and admiration for a true man of God. But there's a significant difference between a historical or biblical treatise with the goal of accurate theology, verse by verse, and a story intended to both entertain and inspire. To make my project work, I have had to take some liberties with my story. Here are some considerations:

All major characters in this story except Mara are mentioned in the biblical account. I included her because I wanted to add more to the personal story of Ziba. The story is told, for the most part, from the viewpoint of Ziba, the servant of Saul (in this case, Jonathan's armor-bearer) who is mentioned in 2 Samuel 9.

Chronology for the story was a compromise between the various chronologies of the time of Saul, based on the work of many biblical historians dating backward from a specific battle fought by King Ahab 150 years later and my desire to make the characters of David and Jonathan, Michal and Ziba consistent with each other. Because there is disagreement as to the ages of Saul, David, and Jonathan, I felt somewhat comfortable adjusting them as necessary for the story. I did, however, try to remain as faithful as I could to the ages referred to in the Bible.

In addition, many incidents happened between Saul and David after the farewell David had with Jonathan and before the battle on Mount Gilboa. However, because this book is about Jonathan rather than David, I have chosen to leave them out.

One of the first challenges I discovered was that the biblical version of the story—like many of the stories in the Bible—is based on incidents without an overarching, continuous story to tie those incidents together. Because of that, I added some literary imagination regarding individuals. There is no evidence that Abner's mother was the witch of Endor, nor that she had contact with Achish, king of Gath. And the Bible doesn't talk about Abner betraying Saul. But all three were real people, and there is no evidence to suggest that what I propose didn't happen. It's included merely for dramatic interest. The plots and subplots and the incidents that tie everything together are included to provide both entertainment and inspiration. I have taken efforts to include all facts that I consider necessary to understand the greater story and how God worked in the lives of all people involved.

Dialogue is relatively accurate, but the retelling of the story required some latitude, especially because I wanted to make their language as modern as possible. Although some may be shocked by the language in the confrontation between Jonathan and Saul in the chapter labeled "Farewell," it is consistent with what the Bible records. See *The Living Bible* for the passage in even more extreme language.

The use of numbers is an issue that may challenge readers. Numbers of armies, such as the two hundred thousand that Saul reportedly raised for the war against the Amalekites, were reduced to be consistent with the limits of the population and archaeological knowledge of that time. Bible scholars are still trying to understand how numbers were used in Old Testament times, but there is an indication that the Hebrew reference for *thousand* may have simply meant *group*.

Finally the references to using iron and bronze. The era in which the story takes place happened at the end of the Bronze Age and the beginning of the Iron Age. Both metals were used during this time. Those blacksmiths who knew how to work with iron were scarce, and the Philistines intended to monopolize that skill by making ironwork and smiths unavailable.

It's not my intention to try to adjust any reader's view of Scripture, and this book should not be viewed as such. My apologies if there is any confusion.

On a final note, despite writing being considered a solitary work, every author knows that the final product is always the result of many people's labors. Here is my short list:

Thanks to the **Rough Writers** gang for enduring my endless questions and reviews for *To the Last Man*. A special thanks goes to **Céleste Perrino-Walker** and **Brisa Ramirez** for adding their critique to the editing process.

Thanks to **Jaime Baldwin** for her work on a map of Israel, and for doing it on short notice.

A hearty thanks goes to **Lloyd Willis**, our resident expert on ancient Israel.

Thanks to my loving wife, **Shelly**, for her endless patience. I love you, sweetheart.

And finally, thanks to my Lord and Savior **Jesus Christ**, who is the beginning and the end of this story.

ISRAEL
IN THE DAYS
OF KING SAUL

PHOENICIANS

CANAANITES

AMMONITES

PHILISTIA

MOABITES

AMALEKITES

• Endor

• Jezreel

• Beth-Shan

• Jabesh-gilead

• Shechem

• Bethel
• Michmash   • Gilgal
Valley of Elah Gibeah • Geba
• Gath   • Socoh   • Ramah
• Jerusalem

Chapter 1

A Conspiracy of Kings

I n southern Canaan, on the fertile plain south of the hill country, yet north of the desert of Negev, lay the mighty walled city of Gath. While many other peoples slept in tents or made structures of wood and mud, Gath stood like solid granite in the flat plain, a monument to the might of the Philistines. Its walls were twenty feet high and ten feet thick. Its gates were two-foot-thick oak beams bound by massive iron straps. And sentinels stood atop the walls, constantly watching the roads in all directions.

Gath was one of five Philistine cities that commanded the fertile plains and coastline of Canaan. Years before, the Philistines had taken the city from the Israelites, and today they protected it jealously. The Philistines—with their heritage of both seamanship and trade—knew its strategic value. They also knew that they had to fight to keep what was theirs.

That was the obvious reason for the parade today. The hot sun baked the parade ground as the three men and their escorts watched the soldiers march by. Armored chariots—their horses protected by sheets of iron; their riders armed with sword, bow, and spear; their wheels tipped with razor-sharp blades—rolled past the small crowd. They were followed by row after row of foot soldiers, their ranks marching in perfect unison, iron-tipped spears rising above them like an advancing forest of death.

"Impressive," said Nahash, king of Ammon, who stood head and

See 1 Samuel 8.

shoulders above the other two. "Philistine armies are always imposing in a parade. Your numbers, your strength—your *iron*—is intimidating enough that no one would dare attack you here on the plains. Your cities are safe for generations to come." His voice came out flat, and it was obvious to the other men that he was being cordial without meaning it.

"Oh come now, Nahash," Agag, king of the Amalekites, said. Where Nahash stood tall and massive like the military man that he was, Agag was a slender man who seemed unassuming, but the other two knew better. Many of Agag's enemies had underestimated him before—and died regretting it. While Nahash's physical prowess was imposing, Agag made up for it in guile.

"We've seen plenty of Philistine chariots before," Agag continued. "They roll through the countryside and even our streets every day. They are enough to intimidate every small child from here to Nineveh. But even with all this might, we all know what our common problem is. All that might, and they couldn't defeat an old man and a group of shepherds and farmers at Mizpah."

Achish nodded, his eyes still watching the soldiers who paraded before them. "Good old Agag, still as astute as ever, eager to get to the point. Well, let's talk about it then." King Achish gestured to them, and they walked away from the procession to take seats in the shade of a stone balcony.

"In the time of our fathers' fathers," Achish began, "this land was disputed by the three of our peoples as well as the Canaanites." Achish paused to let his words sink in. "If you recall the stories, we were all intimidated by them, especially the sons of Anak, giants that they were. As tall as tamarisk trees. They ruled the central hills of Canaan, and we were resigned to living in the lesser land around them. And then something happened."

"*They* happened," Nahash said. "They invaded our land from the east and took it from us."

Agag nodded. "Yes, the people called Israelites arrived. Remember those Canaanites we were afraid of? Where are they today? Destroyed. Defeated. Kicked out of their own country." Nahash and Achish didn't respond.

"What amazes me is that these people are like no other tribe I've ever met," Agag continued. "They have no king. They have no standing army. They barely have towns. They are rabble—and yet they continue to defeat us."

"What do they have that we don't have?" Nahash said.

"I'll tell you what they have," Achish said. "They have a God who takes care of them. They are disorganized, weak, unprepared. But when they're in trouble, when one of us threatens them, they cry out to their God, and then a flood happens, or a great wind comes, or we start seeing armies that aren't there."

"I can fight a standing army," Nahash said. "But how do you fight a God?"

Achish paused before responding. "They haven't always been victors. We've won a few battles. Think about what makes those times unique." The others paused for a long moment before Agag responded.

"It was when they turned away from their God that they became weak," he said. "It was when they depended on themselves. When they became like us."

Achish slowly smiled at the other two. "Exactly. My brothers, I have a plan to finally overcome those wretched Israelites in the hills. A fool-proof plan."

"And what's that?" Nahash asked.

"I'm going to make them just like us," Achish said, still smiling. As the others slowly nodded in agreement, Achish looked over their shoulders at the tall, beautiful woman who stood at the doorway watching them.

❧

"I've thought about your proposal," Achish said to Zephan after the others had left. He'd left the parade in the hot desert sun and retreated to the darker but cooler confines of his conference room, just off the throne room. The thick stone wall was broken by tall, narrow gaps, and slits of light broke the darkness. The slits served as both sources of light as well as kill holes to fire arrows at approaching enemies.

"Let me make sure I understand you correctly," Achish continued, looking at the beautiful woman sitting across the table from him. "You agree to serve as my agent in the land of Israel in exchange for training by our sorcerers here in Gath. Why would you want that?"

"I'm already talented in that respect," Zephan said. "But there's a lot more to be learned. Think of it: if you were to have an agent in Israel who not only would keep you informed but was also a powerful witch, well, think of the possibilities."

Achish smiled grimly. "Without a doubt, you're motivated by the desire for power. We all are. But you do realize that you would be turning your back on the God of Israel *and* allying yourself with forces more dark and powerful than you can imagine. Are you sure you can handle that?"

Zephan smiled broadly. "Believe me, I can and I will."

"Then I see no reason why we can't work something out," Achish said.

Canaan is the crossroads of the world, situated on trade routes between Africa, Asia, and Europe. Roads follow the coast through Philistia from north to south, as do the roads on the east side of the hill country, which travel through Moab and Ammon. But when travelers needed to go from east to west or west to east, they traveled roads that moved through the hill country of Israel. The Israelite towns and villages were scattered across the hillsides, many located at junctions of these roads. Those Israelites who weren't shepherds or farmers made their living as merchants at these locations.

Zephan, the woman at Gath, did not live there. Instead, she traveled back to her home in the north, stopping only along the way at the home of a man called Abner, who also happened to be her son. The conversation at Gath would remain secret, for now, but she knew that she had work to do. It was her intent to change history, and in doing so, guarantee a place in that new history for her son.

The old man known to all of Israel as Samuel the Prophet finished his morning meal and completed his morning devotionals. He then put on his outer robe, kissed his wife goodbye, and exited his humble hut to walk to the gate of Ramah. People came looking for him from all over the countryside, and he'd learned to make it easier for them simply by being somewhere conspicuous. A typical day was filled with him blessing children, watching them play in the field nearby, or helping someone find something they had lost. Today, he knew, would not be a typical day. God had warned him.

Sure enough, he hadn't been seated on his bench for long before he saw a crowd of men walking down the road toward Ramah. He recognized a few of them; Kish was there, as well as Abner, both from Benjamin. He also saw representatives from the other tribes, including Judah and Dan. Some of those he recognized from the battle against the Philistines at Mizpah a few years before. There appeared to be about twenty men, and he might have been alarmed if God hadn't warned him.

He waited until they entered the gates before addressing them.

"Peace be unto you, my brothers," Samuel said.

"Good morning and God bless you, Prophet," Kish said. "We've come to discuss a common need." The men looked at one another as if unsure, but Kish and Abner seemed confident in their address.

"How can I help you?" Samuel said.

"You can help us by giving us a leader," Abner said.

Samuel stared at the young man. "I don't understand. God's our leader."

"We need a king," Abner said, continuing. "We need a king to lead us."

"Why would you say such a thing?" Samuel said, still confused. "Your fathers didn't have a king. Your grandfathers didn't have a king."

"Things have changed," Johan from Judah said.

"What can a king give you that I haven't given you?" Samuel said. "When the Philistines surrounded us with their armies at Mizpah, didn't we have victory? Don't you now live in freedom?"

Kish stepped forward. "Samuel, I was there with you at Mizpah. I remember how you led us. But look at yourself. You're an old man. If we had another battle, could you lead us again? And who'll lead us when you're gone?"

Samuel paused for a moment and then stammered his answer.

"Joel . . . Abijah . . . my sons," he said quietly.

"Your sons are corrupt," Abner said sharply. "They take bribes. They have their favorites. We can't see justice done."

"They're not godly men," Kish added.

Samuel paused again, silently praying to God. Then he began to speak. "But what you're asking. You aren't following the path of God either. You want to be like other nations. You seek a man to lead you . . . instead of God? Are you crazy? Do you have any idea what you're asking?" His voice rose with each question.

"A king will take a tenth of your crops for his own. He'll take your sons to fight in his armies or work on his roads or in his fields. He'll take your daughters to serve in his palace. He'll tell you what to do and where to go and what to say from the day that you crown him king. God has saved you from all of this. And you want to turn your back on God? On me?" He spat the words out. He was offended, hurt, by what they were proposing.

"That's what we want." The words came back bluntly, each word like a knife cutting Samuel as if he'd never done a good thing for his people.

Samuel stood and stared at the men who confronted him. Years before, he'd led them in prayer, and then led them in battle. And now they were confronting him, telling him that they no longer wanted him to lead, that they wanted what Samuel had tried to save them from. He looked from face to face, looking for any sign of support for what he tried to do. But he could tell that they were in agreement.

"So be it," Samuel said. "Go home. I'll talk with my God, and we'll call for you to meet again at Mizpah. God will find you a king."

The men murmured in agreement and turned to walk away. Samuel could tell that they were happy, but he wasn't. He was hurt that after all he'd done they were rejecting him. But more importantly, he knew that the path they'd chosen would lead to a lot of pain and disappointment and in the end, the destruction of Israel.

Chapter 2

The Road to Salvation

Here's another one: Three men meet on the field of battle—an Amalekite, a Canaanite, and a Philistine. The Amalekite shows up in full armor and raises his spear to the sky. 'I have won many battles. I'm not afraid of either of you.' He's promptly run over by the Philistine, who brought his chariot of iron and charges with armored horses right into the Amalekite, cutting him to ribbons in the process. 'I've won hundreds of battles,' the Philistine says. 'And with my chariot, I can't be stopped.' The Canaanite looks at the chariot racing around the field and whistles once. The ground shakes, and a giant Anakim steps forward from the crowd, picking up the chariot and smashing it to the ground and then stomping the life out of the Philistine. The Canaanite says quietly, 'I've never fought in any battles, but with my big friend, of course, I never had to.' "

Abner laughed at his own joke and looked over at his younger cousin, who sat quietly on the oxcart seat. The rolling countryside passed by them slowly as they rode along in the morning light. Saul stared straight ahead, only a wisp of a smile on his face. After a long moment of laughter, Abner quieted.

"Of course, the Canaanites and the Anakim are all gone," Abner added. "We have Joshua to thank for that." Saul didn't respond.

"Oh come on, Gloom and Doom. What's gotten into you?"

Saul shrugged. "You know me. I'm just quiet. I'd have rather stayed home than traveled to Mizpah. I have a field to plow."

See 1 Samuel 10 and 11.

"Field to plow," Abner echoed. "Do you realize what we're about to witness? The first king chosen for Israel. We're finally going to be a real kingdom! Your father was right. This is something you definitely need to be there for."

"Well, Father's already there. The family's represented, so why do I need to be there?" Saul paused and bit his lower lip. "Besides, there's something else."

"What?"

Saul hesitated, struggling to decide whether he should say something. "I already know who'll be chosen."

Abner stared at him, then burst out laughing. "Ahh, so now you're a seer! I suppose you're going to say that you're the chosen one." Abner laughed again.

"I am," Saul said quietly, and Abner stopped laughing.

"You're serious," Abner said.

Saul nodded. "Remember when those two donkeys went missing two weeks ago? I went out with Achim to look for them. I never found them, but I did find the prophet Samuel. He told me that God had chosen me to lead Israel. He even poured oil over my head." Saul turned and looked at Abner, who could tell that Saul wasn't joking.

"So? That's good news! We're about to become a royal family! That's cause for celebration."

"Abner, look at me. I'm no king. I can barely function as a farmer. I lost my father's donkeys. I don't know the first thing about ruling, or leading an army. Why me?"

"Saul, Saul, look at me," Abner said, trying to calm his cousin down. "The first rule to being a wise king is surrounding yourself by those who can give wise counsel. You're not alone in this. As for leading an army, I have experience. I was at the battle of Mizpah. I've led many raids against the Ammonites. I can be your general." He leaned forward and patted Saul's leg.

"Trust me. It'll all work out."

A few hours later, the two of them had joined the rest of the elders from each tribe and family across Israel. The afternoon sun was warm on their shoulders as they met at the high place of worship and meeting on the hill called Mizpah. Samuel was already speaking as they arrived.

"God has shown me that your call for a king was not a rejection of me, but a rejection of Him," Samuel said. "I'll give you one more opportunity to return to a government of being ruled only by God, instead of your insistence that a man rule you as king. A king will tax you, he'll take what's yours, and he'll lead you to die in battle. Is this what you want?"

A ragged cheer went up.

Samuel looked at them grimly. "Very well, then we'll proceed with the casting of lots. I have eleven black stones and one white stone. God will indicate His choice by the tribe to choose the white stone."

Representatives from the twelve tribes of Israel stepped forward, and one by one they reached into the bag that Samuel held, pulling out a stone. Finally they held them up.

"The tribe of Benjamin has been chosen," Samuel announced loudly. "Now we'll choose the clans." Samuel took away stones leaving only enough to represent the six clans within the tribe of Benjamin, and new representatives stepped forward. After a moment, he announced: "The clan of Matri has been chosen. Now the families within the Matri clan should send their representatives up."

Abner watched as his uncle Kish stepped forward and joined the other representatives. A moment later, he heard: "The family of Kish has been chosen. All adult males of this family should come forward."

Abner joined the others up front to draw from the bag. He was disappointed, but not surprised, when he drew out a black stone just like everyone else there. Finally they all compared stones and realized that no one had drawn the white stone. Abner looked at Kish, and both realized that Saul had not come forward.

Samuel asked God where Saul was and learned that he was hiding in the baggage area.

"Here he is," someone shouted from the back of the crowd. They all turned to look as two men pulled Saul from one of the piles of baggage. The tall, young, good-looking man was as white as a sheep. He stood there shaking, held up only by the two men on either side of him.

"Here he is. Here's your king," Samuel said, an edge of sarcasm in his voice.

"Hail King!" the crowd said in unison and bowed before the shaking Saul.

"God have mercy on us all," Samuel said quietly.

The word of Israel's new king spread quickly throughout Canaan, not only in the towns and villages of Israel but in the surrounding kingdoms as well. Nahash, king of Ammon, knew that he'd have to strike fast if he wanted to take advantage of the new king's disorganized start.

Two weeks after the meeting at Mizpah, the massed might of the Ammonite army stood outside the walls of the city of Jabesh-gilead. It wasn't much of a city, for the Israelites had never mastered the art of building high, strong walls or towers. And the city fathers knew that they didn't stand a chance against the powerful Ammonite armed troops.

An entourage, led by Jabek, the chief of the city himself, met Nahash under a banner of truce outside the walls of the city.

"Mighty Nahash, king of Ammon, we surrender before your glorious army," Jabek said. "Make whatever treaty you will, and we will be your subjects."

Nahash sat on his horse, looking down on the small man. "First, show proper respect. Take off your shoes."

Jabek nodded quickly and took off his shoes, looking down at the ground.

"Not enough," Nahash said. "Now take off all your clothes."

Jabek paused. "Your Majesty, the whole city is watching."

"I'm aware of that," Nahash said. "Do it."

Jabek nodded again and began taking off his clothes.

"All of you!" Nahash said to the entourage of men. "Take off all of your clothes. Now."

And in front of the entire city of Jabesh-gilead, the city fathers removed their clothes and stood naked before their conqueror.

"Now about that treaty," Nahash said, smiling at the men below him.

"I'll make a treaty with your city, but under one condition. I'll gouge out the right eye of every one of you. That'll prevent you from ever thinking about fighting back, and it will show the rest of Israel what I think of their new king."

Jabek blanched before Nahash, and the other city fathers gasped. Jabek looked down at the ground, thinking quickly.

"Your Majesty," Jabek began. "Why not show how mighty you really are by confronting this new king on the battlefield? Give us a chance to call for help from Israel. When they arrive, you can once and for all show how mighty you really are."

Nahash stared at the naked men huddled before him. Finally he nodded.

"Very well," he said. "I'll give you seven days. Send out messengers and call for help. If in seven days your help hasn't arrived, we'll put out the right eye of every man, woman, and child in Jabesh-gilead, and we will take your sons and daughters for sacrifice to Moloch, our god of gods."

The men gasped, but Jabek nodded. "That's fair and just, King Nahash."

He looked around him and chose the youngest of the elders who stood around him. "Mathias, prepare to go as our messenger to the new king."

"No."

Jabek turned in surprise at Nahash. The king shook his head atop his horse.

"Not a man," Nahash said. "Her." He pointed across the distance to the city gates where a lone girl stood watching the negotiations. Jabek looked at the young girl, then turned white-faced back to Nahash.

"But she's just a young girl," Jabek stammered. "She's my daughter."

"I know," Nahash said. "I saw you talking to her earlier. Girl, come here." He gestured for the young, dark girl to come to them, and she ran to her father.

"What's your name, girl?" Nahash asked quietly.

"Mara, Your Kingship," the girl replied.

"Mara, I'm giving you a great honor," Nahash said. "Will you ride to the new king of Israel and tell him of your city's need for his help?"

Mara looked at her father, then back at the king. She nodded.

"I'll need to find a horse for her," Jabek said.

"No need," Nahash said. "We'll provide the horse." He gestured behind him, and one of his officers led a horse to them. Mara stepped forward to take the horse's reins, but Nahash held up his hand to stop her.

"But there's one last thing," Nahash said. "We need to make sure that the new king takes you seriously. After all, you're just a girl." He turned again to one of the officers standing by a fire, who reached down and grabbed a burning stick, still black and smoldering.

"I'm being generous in letting your daughter escape this situation," Nahash said. "But I need a sacrifice from her. Captain, put out her right eye."

Jabek shouted and the elders pushed forward, but the soldiers around them pulled out their swords. Two Ammonites grabbed Mara and held her while the captain raised the smoking black stick and forced it into her right eye socket.

Her screams were loud, but short. Two minutes later, she sobbed, and her father held her. The captain who had put out her eye pulled a cloth from his pocket and wrapped it around her head, covering the blind eye.

"Now ride," Nahash said. "Ride to Gibeah as fast as you can. Let the pain drive you forward. Remember your father and your family and your friends here in Jabesh-gilead. Remember those who will die if you fail.

"Ride!"

Chapter 3

King and Champion

I win!" Ziba shouted to Jonathan across the table and jumped to his feet. The burly nine-year-old raised his arms in victory and danced in place, while the younger Jonathan sat quietly, grinning up at his friend.

"See," Jonathan said. "You said you never win at jackal and dogs."

"Well, I don't, usually," Ziba agreed, then paused. "Say, you didn't let me win, did you?"

Jonathan grew serious. "I swear," he said, putting his hand to his chest.

"Yeah," Ziba said. "But what are you swearing?"

"Don't you two have anything better to do than play games? What about your chores? Ziba, I know you can't be done with yours." The boys looked over at Achim, Ziba's father, who stood over a hot fire in the blacksmith pit. Orange flames licked the round stone pit, and black smoke rose into the round hole cut in the center of the ceiling. An assortment of farming implements lay scattered around the fire and next to the stone anvil in the corner.

Ziba looked at the massive man, who wiped sweat from his face and shrugged.

"I got my chores done a couple of hours ago. Mother didn't give me anything else to do, so I helped Jonathan with his, so we'd have time to play jackal and dogs."

"Well, it's almost time for the evening meal. Go see if your mother needs any help."

See 1 Samuel 11.

Ziba started to tell his father he would when a scream interrupted them.

Still holding the scythe he was working on, Achim stood up, and the two boys jumped up from the table. Jonathan pointed to the town center.

"It came from over there." The three of them looked in that direction, as a crowd of people gathered around a young girl on a jet-black horse. Achim climbed out of the pit and strode quickly toward the crowd, with Ziba and Jonathan right behind him.

When they got to the town center, several women helped lower a small girl from a horse to the ground. The girl looked to be a few years younger than Ziba.

Ziba looked closely at the girl. She was pretty and wore robes that appeared higher quality than the rough clothes they wore here in Gibeah, but the white tunic was spattered by black soot and blood. And then she turned her head, and Ziba saw why. The crowd let out a gasp as they saw that the right eye of the girl had been removed. Dried blood and soot were caked on her face. She—or someone else—had tried to cover up the socket with a white bandage, but the blood had soaked through it and had dried. An elderly woman took a clean cloth and wrapped it around that side of her face.

"Come with me," the woman said. "We'll get her cleaned up, and then she needs to rest."

They helped her up and started to carry her away when the girl raised her hand.

"Wait," she said. "I have a message for Saul, son of Kish."

"He's in the fields," the woman told her. "You need to rest and talk to him later."

"I have to talk to him now!" the girl said, her voice filled with surprising power.

As if on command, the crowd parted. Ziba could see Saul, Jonathan's father, leading a yoke of two oxen toward the town, coming from the fields. The crowd stood silently as the tall, commanding presence of Saul came toward them. Finally, he spoke.

"What's going on? What's wrong here?"

The girl stood, teetering for a second and reaching to the woman beside her to gather support, then stood firm.

"I am Mara, daughter of Jabek. I live in Jabesh-gilead. Nahash, the Ammonite, took my eye from me. His army has put Jabesh under siege. The city is peaceful and has no way to protect itself. The fathers have asked for a treaty, saying that they'll obey the order of Nahash. But he doesn't want subjects. He wants slaves. He has told them that when they surrender, he'll put out the right eye of every man, woman, and child in the city and send the children to the fires of Moloch."

A gasp went up, and immediately the women in the crowd began to wail.

"Quiet!" Saul shouted. "Quiet, all of you!"

"My father sent me for help. Nahash agreed to let me go, but only if my eye was taken so that others would see that he was serious."

Saul stepped forward and tenderly placed his massive hand on Mara's blood-caked head. Mara looked at Saul, and Ziba could see desperation mixed with anger on her face.

"Saul of Gibeah, you've been anointed king of Israel," she continued. "Your tribe has a special bond with the people of Jabesh-gilead. We're calling for your help. How will you respond?"

His hand still resting on her head, Saul's lips moved. Ziba could barely hear the words: "How will I respond . . . ?"

Ziba watched the expression on Saul's face slowly turn from confusion and indecision to a hard, almost terrifying grimace. He reached over and took the scythe that Achim still carried, and then he turned toward the two black plowing oxen behind him, still tethered together with a wooden yoke. With one smooth motion, Saul slashed the sharp scythe across the throat of one ox, and then the other. The front legs of the mighty animals collapsed beneath them. Blood spurted and sprayed everyone within six feet of the two oxen. Finally the two beasts lay in a gathering pool of their own blood.

The crowd stood stunned, many of them splashed by the hot, red blood of the two animals. A second later, most took a step backward, wondering if Saul had lost his mind. In the meantime, Saul had dropped the scythe and picked up an ax. Oblivious to the blood that flew everywhere, he chopped into the two dead animals, cutting off their heads, then each of their powerful legs.

A few people had left the spectacle, but most remained fascinated by Saul's action. After cutting the animals apart, he turned to the crowd. Blood was everywhere on his tunic and face and hair.

"I need twelve volunteers," he said to the crowd. "One for each of the twelve tribes."

Murmuring broke out, but after a few moments, twelve young men stepped forward.

"This young woman has lost her eye and risked her life to get this message to us," Saul said. "Each of you will take a piece of these animals and go to a tribe of Israel. This is the message I want you to deliver: 'This is what will be done to your oxen if you don't follow Saul and Samuel.' Now go. We meet at Bezek in two days' time."

For a people who had strict rules about touching animal blood, the sight of Saul—and many of those in the community—shocked them and filled them with fear. Ziba watched Saul as the crowd broke up and saw that he was suddenly telling many people what to do. There was a feeling of restrained panic throughout the town, a feeling Ziba had never seen before. He turned to look at his father and saw that he'd returned to the blacksmith pit. Jonathan had disappeared as well, and a moment later, Ziba saw that he'd been snatched up by some of the men of the village.

"Father," Ziba said, running back to the pit. "What's going on?"

Achim was loading his bronze utensils into a two-wheeled cart. At first, he seemed not to hear what Ziba was saying. Ziba saw stress on his face that he'd never seen before.

"Father? Father?" Finally Achim paused in what he was doing.

"Son, gather up my tools. They'll be needed."

"Needed?" Ziba echoed. "Needed for what?"

Achim grabbed Ziba by the shoulders and looked into his face. "We're going to war. Now help me."

The two of them worked until well after dark, loading pitchforks, scythes, axes, and sharp wooden spears into the wagon. When it got too dark to see, women went throughout the village carrying torches to illuminate their work. Finally, they took a break to eat together. A big pot of lentil and mutton stew was heating over a central fire. Everyone—including Ziba—was given a big bowl of stew with a large chunk of bread. Ziba ate his hungrily and then looked around the fire for Jonathan. The younger boy was nowhere to be seen.

Ziba did see Mara, the girl from Jabesh-gilead who had bravely ridden into town on the black horse. She'd been cleaned up, and a fresh bandage had been placed over her injury. She sat opposite Ziba, eating stew and staring at the fire. Ziba watched her in awe, wondering if he would have had the courage she had found to ride forty miles through the wilderness after having her eye put out. While he watched her, she glanced up at him, and Ziba quickly looked away. He waited a few moments, looking around the circle by the fire, then looked at her again. To his embarrassment, she was still looking at him, a small smile on her lips. He smiled quickly, then looked away again.

The wagon was loaded soon after the evening meal was complete, and Ziba helped his father hook up the oxen to the tongue of the wagon. Exhausted, and unused to such late hours, Ziba crawled into a small space in the back of the wagon at Achim's prompting and was soon asleep.

A bump and a flash of sunlight awoke Ziba the next morning. Achim sat on the small seat in front of the wagon, directing the team of oxen. Ziba sat up and looked around. A line of men and women followed them, and as Ziba turned, he could see that the line stretched forward out of sight as well.

"Where are we?" Ziba said.

"Good morning, son," Achim said. "We're on the east side of the mountains. Soon we'll be passing through Gilgal."

Ziba looked at the line of people. "Are all of these people going to war? All of them going to fight?"

"War, yes. Fight, no," Achim said. "It takes many people to fight a war, with only a few of them frontline warriors. We need people to feed the army, others to help the wounded, and still others," he gestured to the wagon, "to make the weapons that'll be used in battle. I do my part by providing weapons for the soldiers."

"Weapons?" Ziba echoed. "All I see are tools from farming. How can you fight a battle with sticks and scythes?"

"Ahh, true," Achim said. "These are tools for farming. They're not swords and shields. But the real power in battle comes from Jehovah. If you have Jehovah on your side, it doesn't matter what else you have. You could have a rock and could take down a giant in thick armor. It all depends on God's plan."

⚹

Achim reached into a sack he had next to his left foot and handed Ziba a chunk of bread. Ziba took it and climbed over the back of the driver's seat to sit next to his father. He bit into the crusty bread while he watched the people in front of them follow the rugged road toward the town of Gilgal.

Ziba had never been to a big city and was eager to see what Gilgal was like. But they didn't enter Gilgal. Instead, the winding trail of men and women, horses and oxen, moved around the tall walls of the city as if it were a giant stone that was in their way. Ziba sighed as he watched the city disappear behind them.

But the land around him was different. His small town of Gibeah was set in the mountains where people mostly raised sheep or scrabbled for a plot of land to raise a few vegetables. This land was flat and rich with wheat and barley. Water from the nearby river ran in canals to feed the crops.

"Father, this is a good land," Ziba said. "Look at it! We could raise cattle and sheep here, or farm vegetables or wheat or whatever we want. Why don't we live here?"

Achim stared ahead at the oxen as he continued to drive the cart. "This is a fertile land, and many people know it. That's why we're going to war. The Ammonites feel that they own this land, even though God gave it to us. We have to take it back from them."

"But after we take it back, we could live here, couldn't we?"

Achim smiled and shook his head. "Our family is a family of

servants, born to serve the tribe of Benjamin. And Benjamites live in the highlands. Besides, it's a lot easier to keep what you own up there than down here."

"Why is that?"

"You haven't had to deal with the armies of other people before. Ammonites and Elamites and Amalekites armor themselves up with sword and shield to come and take what they want. But when you have armor on you, you move more slowly and it's hard to climb into the high places. Those are the places that protect us."

"But you're a blacksmith, Father. You can make swords and shields and even armor for our men so that they can protect their land and their family."

"I work with bronze," Achim said. "And bronze is to iron as butter is to a knife. No one in all of Israel has learned the secret of making iron. That's why I travel to Philistia once a month. I have a couple of blacksmith friends in Gath that I'm hoping someday will teach me what they know."

"Why don't they teach you now?"

"If their leaders found out that an Israelite had learned the secret of iron, they would have their heads and my head too," he said grimly. "It's the greatest secret they own."

He paused. "You've never seen a chariot, and I hope you never have to. A chariot is a wagon covered with iron. Two horses pull it, and two men ride in it. One drives the horses; the other is either an archer or a spearman. They move fast and usually are deadly accurate. And there's no way to stop them."

Ziba tried to visualize what his father described, but couldn't. "I'd like to see such a chariot."

"I pray you don't. The Philistines have them—thousands of them— along with armored troops who are highly trained." Achim frowned, then his voice brightened. "But they can't climb hillsides and run mountain passes. That's why we've been able to live in peace all these years."

"We're like a cat in a tree with dogs on the ground," Ziba said, smiling. "They can't get us!"

"Exactly, my son," Achim said, his voice dark again. "We're a cat caught in a tree. I only pray that our new king, Saul, will draw the country together so that this cat can overcome the dogs."

The miles passed quickly as Ziba looked at the countryside. He looked for signs of farmers working in the fertile fields, but the acreage was empty. The road came over a rise, and they came to a broad valley that was uncultivated and had tall grass growing in all directions. A grove of trees stood along the edge of the valley.

"Welcome to Bezek," Achim said to his son.

"But there's nothing here," Ziba said.

"You're right. It's just a crossroads. But it's secluded and large enough for the soldiers of Israel to gather. And it's within marching distance of Jabesh-gilead. I suspect that Saul plans on waiting for the others to arrive here, and then marching the rest of the way tonight."

People were gathered there already. The group that Achim and Ziba were with got off the road and started to set up camp. Ziba helped Achim set up their small tent and start a fire where he could continue to work on weapons.

"See if you can find us something to eat," Achim told Ziba, and Ziba wandered off.

As the sun rose in the sky, others continued to arrive in the vale. Before long, Ziba realized that there were more people than he'd ever been around. He found a group of women with cooking pots and convinced one of them to give him two bowls of porridge. He had just turned to head back when he saw Mara, the girl from Jabesh, sitting shyly behind one of the women.

"Hi," Ziba said to the girl.

"Hello," she said quietly.

"I'm surprised they let you come along," Ziba said.

"I'm the only person that the Ammonites will let through the lines. I'm the messenger."

"Well, I think you're awfully brave."

"Thanks."

"Does it hurt?" Ziba asked, gesturing toward his own eye.

"Sometimes. The women give me an herb poultice to put on it, and that helps a lot. But sometimes it still hurts."

"Mara?" they heard a man's voice say. "Come with me."

They turned to see a man dressed in thick leather armor. He wasn't as tall as Saul or Ziba's father, Achim, but he was broad across the shoulders. His hair was black and cut short, like that of the Philistines that Ziba had seen. He wore a short sword in a scabbard on his belt and carried a six-foot spear with a bronze tip. His face held what looked like a permanent scowl and a scar that went from the tip of his nose to the bottom of his left ear. Ziba immediately felt uncomfortable around the man.

Mara got up from where she was sitting and followed the man through the crowd. Ziba forgot all about the porridge he was carrying and followed them. They wound through masses of people until they came to a white tent that was pitched at the edge of the vale, right beside a giant oak tree. They started to enter the tent, but the man held up his hand and stopped them at the entrance.

"Wait here," he said. The flap was opened, and Ziba could see inside to the dark interior. Suddenly he saw a familiar face.

"Jonathan!" he said. Jonathan stepped out of the tent and into the sunlight.

"Hi, Ziba!"

"Jonathan, this is Mara. She's the girl who brought the message and got her . . . her . . ."

"Eye," she said. "The word is eye."

"Yeah, I know," Jonathan said. "I was there when my father killed the oxen."

"Wasn't that something?" Ziba said. "I've never seen so much blood!"

"Mara, what you did was very brave," Jonathan said.

"I already told her that," Ziba said. "Come on, let's go explore the camp."

"I can't," Jonathan said. "Abner says I have to learn to be a prince now."

"Abner? Who's Abner?"

"The man with the spear? The one who brought the two of you here? He's my father's cousin and his new general."

"General? He's really a general?"

Jonathan shrugged. "He says he is. He's been to Philistia—lots of times, actually—and he says we have a lot to learn about being a kingdom. He and his mother want to show us how to be just like the royal family there."

Ziba frowned. "I don't think we want to do that, do we?"

Jonathan shrugged again. "All I know is that they won't let me do the stuff I used to do. They say I'm a prince, so I can't play with the other kids.

"They say I have to learn how to replace my father as king someday. All I can say is being the son of a king is not much different than being the son of a farmer, only a lot more boring."

"There you are," Ziba heard behind him, and Achim stepped up, placing his hand on Ziba's head. "You've forgotten about your starving father, have you?" He reached down and squeezed Ziba's shoulder, and Ziba responded by handing his father the bowl of porridge he had for him.

"Hello, Mara," said Achim. "I see you're doing better."

"Yes, sir," she said.

"Mara's been summoned before the king," the man known as Abner said, returning to the tent entrance. "We need to get a message to the people inside." He motioned for Mara to enter, then turned to Ziba and Achim. "Boy, you will have no more contact with Prince Jonathan. He has a lot of training to do."

Abner straightened up and squared his shoulder against Achim.

"Don't you have weapons to make for our army?" he said quietly, but with an edge to his voice.

Achim stared back at Abner, not backing down. Then he turned to Ziba without taking his eyes off of the other man.

"Come on, son. We have work to do."

"I don't like that man," Ziba said quietly as they wandered through the crowd.

"To tell you the truth, I don't like him much either," said Achim. "He reminds me too much of the people of Gath. Selfish, jealous, ruthless."

"I wish that Saul had chosen someone else to be his general."

"No one around here knows much about warfare or running a kingdom. And Abner and Saul seem to have a special bond. They probably think Abner and his mother, Zephan, know what a king should do. You'll notice that even though Saul was recognized as king, he still works on his farm. But this battle may change things."

Achim gestured around him, and Ziba noticed that the vale had grown much busier since he'd gone to get food. More and more people continued to gather in the valley, coming in from three directions. It was a collection of common people, many of them obviously either farmers or shepherds. But there were merchants and other folk as well.

"There are thousands here now, and by nightfall we'll have tens of thousands. All of them have answered the call to follow the king of Israel. If Saul is successful tomorrow, things'll change."

They continued to work on weapons, and more and more men came by their tent looking for something to carry into battle. When it grew dark and the torches appeared, Achim was called away. After about an hour, he returned.

"King Saul has sent Mara back to Jabesh-gilead with the message, 'By midday tomorrow we will deliver you.' She left about an hour ago. There are thousands and thousands of men ready to go to battle tomorrow morning. I've done my duty and provided as many as possible with weapons. Early tomorrow we leave. I have something to show you. Now rest."

Ziba lay down in the tent and tried to sleep. A few hours later, while it was still very dark, his father woke him. He dressed and followed his father, leaving their tent and wagon behind.

Achim traveled directly west and soon discovered a path that wound up a hillside and up to a cliff. They followed the path along the cliff edge for about an hour. Then Achim lay down in the tall grass and gestured for Ziba to do the same. They lay on the edge of the cliff and looked down into farmland. In the center of a valley was a walled city. Surrounding it, Ziba could see many tents with a few campfires that had died in the late night.

"That's Jabesh-gilead," Achim said quietly. "Watch the tree line."

The two of them lay silently in the early-morning darkness, waiting for something to happen. Then Achim raised his hand and pointed.

"There," he said, pointing to the eastern side of the valley. "And there, and there." He pointed out dark shapes moving far below them, figures coming from the tree line and moving into the valley, moving into the sleeping army of the Ammonites.

The few shapes became many; the many became a flood. What Ziba had strained to see at first now became obvious to him. What surprised him was how many had come into the camp without the Ammonites reacting. Finally he heard a shout and metal clashing against metal.

"To arms! To arms!" he heard shouted. And as the morning sun rose, he heard more and more voices rising in alarm.

"They know we're here," Ziba said.

"Too late," his father said. "We have thousands in their camp. By the time they rise and prepare for battle, it'll be over."

The morning sun rose red, scattering scarlet rays across the growing battlefield. The Ammonites were being attacked on three sides, and Ziba watched silently as man after man was killed in front of his eyes by the charging army of Israel.

"Son, many people talk about the glory of battle, but those who do often have never raised their hand against an enemy or run for their lives, praying that they'll live to see another day.

"It's important for you to know that war is a dirty, terrible business. The only glory that comes from war is that which goes to God for letting you live another day. War should be avoided at all costs. But if it can't be avoided, then you have to go in prepared to win."

Ziba nodded, unsure of why his father was telling him this.

"Life as we know it's about to change, Ziba. You have a choice. You can become a blacksmith like me. Or you can do what you can to make the kingdom of Saul and his family successful. What will it be?"

Ziba frowned, then looked down at the battle below them.

"Jonathan will need my help," he said. "I see that now. I want to do whatever I can to help him."

Achim nodded. "That's what I thought you would say." He rolled over and looked up at the sky.

"Saul will still listen to me, at least for the time being. And Jonathan will need an armor-bearer, someone to protect him and help him carry the load."

He rolled back over and looked at his son.

"You'll be Jonathan's armor-bearer. And your fate will be tied to that of Jonathan forever."

Chapter 4

Encounter at Geba

Jonathan and Ziba pushed silently on their bellies through the grass until they could see over the edge of the hillside. The evening was still, and as the sun set over their left shoulders, they moved as quietly as they could so they wouldn't be noticed by the Philistine guards below.

Saul had spent the past seven years training a force to respond to outside threats, such as what had happened in Jabesh-gilead. That same seven years had given both Jonathan, as the crown prince, and Ziba, as his armor-bearer and bodyguard, the time to grow into young men. Jonathan looked much like his father, tall and slender, but with a commanding presence that caught the respect of those he spoke to. He was just old enough to sprout a beard, which grew in wisps on the end of his chin but nowhere else. His eyes were grey and sharp, constantly searching around him but with an innate intelligence that people respected.

Ziba now looked more like his father, Achim—half a foot shorter, but with powerful arms and shoulders, most of it from the years of learning his father's trade when he wasn't carrying armor and weapons and hiking long distances in training for the army. His leg muscles were thick; where Jonathan was built to be a runner, Ziba was built to be a weightlifter. His light brown hair curled around his shoulders, and his face was still clean of hair, even though he was two years older than Jonathan.

See 1 Samuel 13.

A clearing stood before them, with four watchtowers overshadowing a large meadow that had been cleared for a greater area of vision. Ziba found that the spot they'd chosen was directly across from one of the towers, with a second far to the east, nearer the ravine. Two others stood off to the west, on the other side of the road that led to Gibeah.

Beyond the watchtowers and the scattered torches lay a ten-foot-tall wooden fence. Beyond that, Ziba knew, lay the Philistine garrison of Geba. They lay and looked at the layout of the defenses, and then Jonathan pushed away from the edge and retreated, with Ziba following closely and silently behind.

Jonathan said nothing until they reached the bottom of the small hill and were back to their own forces.

"Just as you described it, Ziba," Jonathan said. "You'd make a good scout."

Ziba shook his head. "Thanks, but I'm kept plenty busy protecting your backside." He added quickly, "That is, your *royal* backside, Prince."

Jonathan grinned. "You never let me forget that, do you? Seven years as my armor-bearer and you act more like a mother than you do a warrior."

Ziba's eyes narrowed and his smile disappeared. "Just let me get close to those donkey-eating Philistines, and you'll see what kind of warrior I can be."

Jonathan slapped Ziba on the shoulder. "Don't worry, Ziba. If your father is there at the garrison, we'll get him out. Regardless of what Abner says."

Ziba smiled. "Like I said, a prince trumps a general any day. Besides, when he and your father went off to Bethel, he left you in charge. Didn't he? That says to me that you're the boss. Including taking charge of the rescue of a worthy servant in the employ of the royal family."

"Who just happens to be the father of my trusty armor-bearer and bodyguard," Jonathan added.

Ziba shrugged. "There is that. There's also that other thing—the fact that we don't have any weapons. I mean, other than the occasional bronze ax or sickle. How do you propose we take on a garrison of armored Philistines with no weapons?"

Jonathan winked. "I have an idea about that. And if we're successful, we might get a few of those fancy iron swords, spears, and shields we're always hearing about."

As he finished those words, the two of them reached the line of Israelite soldiers standing at the edge of the trees just east of the road to Gibeah. One big man with an ear cut off stepped forward. It was Uthai, the sergeant of arms for the division of men that Saul had left with Jonathan. The man saluted Jonathan by striking his leather-armored chest with a balled fist.

Jonathan nodded at him in reply. He stepped forward and spoke quietly to Uthai.

"OK, here's the plan. We're not here to attack the Philistines. We're here to rescue someone. But the Philistines don't know that. So your job is to draw attention to the division here south of the garrison while Ziba and I sneak in to rescue Achim."

Uthai stared back at the two of them without speaking.

"Something wrong, Uthai?" Jonathan asked. "Speak up, because in a minute, it'll be too late."

Uthai paused, then shook his head. "I don't like this, Your Majesty."

"Uthai," Jonathan said, slapping his shoulder. "I don't like it either. But the first thing you learn when you're a warrior is that you have to do things you don't like to do. I don't want anyone hurt or killed. I just want you to get their attention. I figure some of those close-order drills you're famous for should do the trick. Don't you agree?"

Uthai nodded, a slight smile coming to his face. "I believe the men and I can manage that."

"Just make plenty of noise and make them think there are three times as many of you," Jonathan said over his shoulder. "When that draws them out from the garrison, Ziba and I'll make our move. Most importantly, Uthai, make sure no one gets hurt."

Jonathan and Ziba slipped back into the darkness, and Uthai turned to the troops.

"Attention, troops! Ready for close order! Form ranks!" he shouted.

Ziba and Jonathan moved as quietly and quickly as they could in the darkness. They heard the voice of Uthai behind them. Ziba cringed, hoping that some random arrow would not find Uthai in the shadows. This whole adventure was a rescue that he'd intended to do alone, but his pledge to the family had made him tell Jonathan of his intentions. Jonathan had done nothing until Saul and Abner had left Gibeah with their men. But when he was officially in charge, he wasted no time rallying the men to go into battle. The trouble was, after seven years of training, they had lots of discipline but still very few weapons. Ziba knew that Jonathan could justify the raid by saying that as a weapons maker, Achim was worth the risk. But Ziba knew that Jonathan's feelings and motivations went far beyond that. Achim was family, just as Ziba was.

They passed the spot where they'd climbed the hillside earlier, and continued sweeping around to the east in a wide semicircle. Soon they came to the path that ran along the upper edge of the ravine. Beyond them, just beyond the light of the nearest torch, was the easternmost lookout tower. Jonathan and Ziba waited in the darkness for something to happen.

A few minutes later, a shout went up from the garrison. Philistines began running out of the gate in the middle of the wooden fence. Ziba watched the men in the lookout tower turn to look down the south road toward Gibeah, the road where Uthai and his soldiers were marching in close-order drill. Jonathan tapped Ziba on the shoulder, and the two of them crept silently past the tower and through the open gate and into the fenced area.

Ziba discovered that the garrison towers and fence were intended to keep armies out of the area, but once one was inside, it was pretty easy to get around. The two of them followed the line of the wooden fence around to the west and directly to the edge of the ravine. To the left, Ziba could see the low form of the garrison barracks. Behind that, he saw a lower building that appeared at least partially buried underground. Outside the entrance stood a single soldier, who was apparently guarding something. Ziba suspected that it was the entrance to the garrison jail.

They stood in the shadow of the fence, about fifty feet away, and considered what to do. As all Philistines were, the man was heavily armored, while Jonathan and Ziba wore the typical leather armor of the Israelites. Ziba's first inclination was to shoot the soldier with an arrow. But a shot at night would very likely only bounce off the iron scales, making the guard angry, and would be very, very loud. Jonathan silently tapped on Ziba's shoulder and through gestures gave Ziba the outline of a plan. Ziba paused, then nodded. Jonathan backed into the shadows and crept closer to the ravine, while Ziba worked his way back in the direction of the barracks.

Ziba waited until the guard was looking the other direction, then crossed the open area to the barracks. Then he straightened himself and began walking rather stiffly toward the guard, as if he were expected.

Just as they hoped, in the dark the guard mistook Ziba for one of his friends.

"Did you save me any dinner?" the guard said. Ziba said nothing, but continued walking toward the guard.

"Did you? Hey, answer me, you son of a dog," the guard continued. Ziba gritted his teeth and continued walking toward the armored soldier. Finally, Ziba was close enough that the soldier realized that he was an enemy soldier. He opened his mouth to shout out a warning, but at that instant, Jonathan appeared from behind him. He ran a sharp bronze blade across the Philistine's throat while holding the other hand over his mouth. The guard's eyes grew wide as blood poured down his front, then he collapsed silently to the ground.

Ziba reached down and pulled a ring of keys from the guard's belt. Grabbing a nearby torch, he turned and unlocked the big padlock on the door to the sunken building. After a short amount of fumbling, he unlatched the heavy wooden door and opened it wide. He raised the torch and looked inside.

The simple jail consisted of a hole in the ground reinforced by rocks with a roof of wooden beams. One end of the jail featured the heavy door. Ziba looked inside at the one room and saw his father, lying on the ground.

"Father! We've come to rescue you."

"So you have, so you have!" Achim said, struggling to stand up and walk toward the door. "But we have to rescue my friend as well." He motioned at a very old man with a bandaged head who shared the jail with him.

"Who's your friend?" Ziba said.

"A Philistine, but don't worry. He's agreed to share the secrets of iron with us."

Ziba stepped forward and helped Achim out the door. Then he reached out to the old man.

"I'm Ziba," he said, holding out his hand.

"He can't answer you. When they found out that he was willing to help us, they cut out his tongue. But he still wants to help. His name is Leal."

The old man smiled up at Ziba and extended a shaking hand, and Ziba took it. They exited the jail and joined Jonathan, who had pulled out his bow and stood ready to defend against any soldiers. Ziba led Achim and Leal into the shadow of the fence and to the edge of the gate. Ziba stepped forward to watch the gate. When he saw that the sentries at the towers were looking elsewhere, he motioned for the others. Jonathan started toward the gate but stopped when a heavy man came out of the barrack door without a shirt on.

"Guards!" he shouted. "We have—"

Jonathan's arrow stopped him in midsentence. He looked down at his bare chest with the shaft of an arrow sticking out of it. He looked up at Jonathan again, then collapsed.

"Run!" Jonathan shouted.

Arrows began to fly from all four of the lookout towers. Ziba realized that Leal would not be able to keep up with them, so he ran back inside the gate to throw the thin old man over his shoulder.

The four of them stopped in their tracks when they heard a horn sound from above them in one of the towers, and an answer come bugling back from the darkness directly ahead of them. Half a minute later, a mob of Philistines in iron armor came rushing back toward them, apparently to protect the garrison.

Ziba turned to Jonathan, who immediately shouted, "Back inside!"

They ran past the body of the man with the arrow in his chest and into the barracks, hoping that nobody else was there. They were alone. The roar of the Philistines coming toward them grew louder, and then another sound was added. Ziba hesitated, listening closely from inside the barracks, then realized that it was the sound of their own troops.

In the meantime, Jonathan had stepped into the armory in the next room and picked up two iron-tipped spears, a sword, and a round shield. He tossed a spear to Ziba and one to Achim. He nodded for Ziba to follow him but gestured palm-out for Achim to stay.

"I can fight," the older man said.

"I know," Jonathan said. "But you'll be needed to protect your friend, whether Israel or Philistia wins. Right now, he's worth protecting."

Achim nodded and took a tighter grip on the spear that he held.

Jonathan and Ziba charged through the door and toward the gate. What they saw on the other side of the gate, however, made them pause. In their hurry to get back to the garrison, the Philistines had broken ranks and had forgotten about the Israelites. Because they were not heavily armored, the soldiers of Israel could not only run faster than the Philistines but outmaneuver them, and they were fresher when they did make contact. Using axes, wooden stakes, bronze sickles, heavy rocks, and even their bare hands, the Hebrews overcame the hundred or so Philistines in the clearing outside the gate and killed them all.

The sentries in the towers were another problem, though. With two men in each of four towers, loaded with arrows, they began to shoot any Israelites within range of their bows. The towers were well lit, and the ground outside had torches lit on high poles and on the walls. Jonathan shouted at the men outside.

"Put out the torches!" he yelled at Uthai, who stood just outside the gate, using a shield taken from a dead Philistine to protect himself from the hail of arrows.

Uthai nodded in understanding, then yelled for the others to put them out. Soon, only the torches on the towers were still lit. It was harder for the sentries to hit soldiers in the dark. In the meantime, a row of Israelite archers made short work of the sentries in the towers.

"Get some of our men up there," Uthai shouted, gesturing to the towers. "Scout the area, and make sure we got everyone."

Jonathan trotted up to the sergeant and gripped his arm.

"Not what I'd intended, but I'll take it," he said grimly. "Any idea on casualties?"

Uthai shook his head. "Give me a few minutes, and I'll tell you. I think it looks worse than it is." Uthai looked down.

"Sorry to disobey your orders, my prince, but your father—"

"Yes, I know," Jonathan said, interrupting. "He'd have you boiled alive if anything happened to me. Well, we got what we came for, and then some."

"I'll send messengers to the king in Hebron, letting him know of our victory here. I'll also send out skirmishers to make sure no message gets back to Philistia."

Jonathan shook his head. "They'll know soon enough. Why worry about it?"

"I'm afraid that we've awakened a lion by tweaking its tail."

Uthai immediately set up defenses against any counterattack. Jonathan and Ziba made sure that the armory and the dead Philistines helped arm as many Israelite soldiers as possible, even though the garrison held only a hundred men, and Jonathan had one thousand troops following him. An hour later, they all tried to get some rest.

It wasn't until late the following afternoon that Uthai returned to Jonathan, his face drawn into a grim line.

"Trouble?" Jonathan asked. Uthai nodded.

"Despite our efforts, the garrison sent horsemen to Gath. Philistia has already turned out its army—its whole army. It appears they take it very seriously when someone attacks one of their garrisons."

"We should have attacked them years ago," Jonathan muttered.

"Your father had his reasons for holding off any challenge to the Philistines. That man you shot with the arrow was the garrison commander. He's also a cousin to King Achish of Gath. They are out for blood."

"How many are we talking about?" Ziba asked.

"King Saul sent a runner from Hebron, saying that they have at least three thousand chariots."

"Three *thousand*?" Ziba echoed.

"Each of them unstoppable. And soldiers like the sands of the sea. Your father asks that I take command here. You and your armor-bearer are to meet him in Gilgal. That'll be the rally point for the armies of Israel."

"I hope we have as many turn out as we did for the battle in Jabesh-gilead," Ziba said.

"If we don't, we're all in trouble," Uthai muttered.

It took until almost midnight for Jonathan and Ziba to arrive in Gilgal, even with fast horses. The community had served as the staging area for the invasion of Canaan generations ago and since had been accepted by Israel as the rally point for any danger that beset the country. Jonathan and Ziba expected to find the camp filled to overflowing with volunteers from the twelve tribes. Instead, it was relatively quiet. Jonathan and Ziba drew their horses up to a makeshift stable that had been assembled, and a page took the animals away.

"Where's my father?" Jonathan asked a soldier standing there, who gestured toward the king's white tent on the other side of the meadow. Ziba followed Jonathan through the camp. He expected to hear the usual loud voices and boisterous talk, accompanied by some singing. Instead, the men who camped here were quiet, with a somber mood overshadowing the camp. As they walked toward the white tent of Saul, more than once Ziba noticed that men avoided looking at them.

"Do you get the feeling we're in trouble?" Ziba said under his breath.

Jonathan nodded. "Don't worry. Father will be upset with me. You were just doing your job."

Ziba sighed. "Through thick or thin, count me in. Whatever you do, I'm with you."

Jonathan smiled thinly. "That rhyme was great when we were kids. But we're not kids anymore."

"Regardless, my prince," Ziba said, "your fate is mine."

Jonathan nodded as they came to the tent. "Thanks, Ziba."

Two guards stood outside the tent with bronze spears crossed to prohibit anyone from entering. Jonathan stepped close to one of them.

"Is there a reason why the crown prince is prevented from seeing his father, the king?"

"King Saul is meeting with General Abner, Your Highness," the guard said. "I was instructed to let no one in."

"I doubt very much that includes me," Jonathan said, inching closer to the soldier. "Get out of my way."

The guard stared at Jonathan for a moment, then flinched. He pulled his spear back, and the other guard did as well. Jonathan stepped forward, and Ziba began to follow him. The guard stepped in front of Ziba.

"Not you," the guard said.

Ziba stepped within an inch of the older guard. Scratches from their encounter at Geba had left the side of his face red with blood. He narrowed his eyes, and his face became stone.

"I'm the bodyguard to the prince. I go where he goes. I'll kill to protect him. And I'm very good at what I do. If you don't believe me, just keep doing what you're doing."

Once again, the guard wavered and stepped out of the way. Ziba followed Jonathan into the tent. Jonathan grinned slightly at Ziba, who raised his eyebrows. Ziba had always been good at bluffing.

As they entered, they noticed that King Saul was looking over maps with Abner, his general.

"Overall, it doesn't look good," Abner was saying. "The Philistines are determined to chase us out of the central passes, and every community within twenty miles of there. According to our scouts, they have tens of thousands and they're well armored and supplied. They intend to cut our country in half. They already control the coastline. If they take over the passes, anyone who needs to go from south to north will have to go completely around to the Jordan Valley. And it'll be only a matter of time before they take that too. We need to act right away."

"No," Saul said. "Samuel said he'd be here. We have to wait for Samuel."

"What's the value of an animal sacrifice and the pious prayer of some prophet compared to striking when strategy calls for it? If we wait too long, they'll be entrenched, and we'll never be able to root them out."

Saul stared at the map and continued to shake his head. But as Ziba watched him, he could see doubt in the king's face.

"He'll come," Saul said, still staring at the map.

Not only did Samuel not come, but the expected reinforcements from the twelve tribes failed to come as well. Scouts brought reports of Israelites running in fear of the massive armored Philistine army crossing the mountains from the coastline. Many hid in caves, and others crossed the Jordan to hide in neighboring countries. What was most discouraging were reports of hundreds of Israelites joining the ranks of the Philistines. There had always been interaction between the tribes of the central mountains and the organized Philistine cities on the coast. And the Philistines encouraged it by making sure they retained a monopoly on important trades, such as blacksmithing, jewelry-making, and wheelwrights. Now many of the relationships originally developed in business had proved to be stronger than the relationship they had to their kin.

Ziba didn't worry about the garrison at Geba. Uthai was one of the best-trained and most-experienced soldiers that the army of Saul had. That was the reason why Saul had made him second to his son. What worried Ziba was if they would be able to bring any aid to those thousand men anytime soon. Challenging a garrison of a hundred men was one thing; holding back tens of thousands of fresh troops and chariots was close to impossible.

By prior arrangement, the army of Saul was required to wait seven days until Samuel arrived to ask for God's blessing on their efforts. But as the week wore on, not only did fresh troops stop arriving at Gilgal; each night more and more seemed to disappear from the ranks. And all that time, Jonathan and Ziba watched Abner continue to urge Saul to lead what was left of his army into battle. Finally, on the seventh day, scouts brought word that the Philistines had stopped their forward advance.

Saul stared at the map, then stood and walked to the open flap of the tent. Staring out, he said: "Any word of Samuel? Has anyone seen him?"

"No, my king," said a scout standing by the door.

Saul hesitated, then nodded. "Prepare the sacrifice. If Samuel isn't here to do it, I guess I'll have to take care of it."

Jonathan took a step forward. "But father, he promised to come."

"We can't wait all day," Abner interjected. "We need to move now."

"Just a little longer—"

"Silence!" Saul roared at his son. "You forget who's king."

"I thought my place was to learn how to be king and lead God's people someday."

"If we don't do something, God won't have any people," Saul said, shaking his head. He turned to the guards. "Take him and keep him somewhere safe."

Two guards stepped forward to escort Jonathan out. Ziba stepped forward to intervene, but Jonathan shook his head slightly, and Ziba stepped back.

A few minutes later, an altar of twelve round stones had been prepared, and Saul stepped forward in front of the few hundred remaining soldiers in a gathering place outside. He took a knife and cut the throat of a lamb, then laid it on the altar. Then he took a torch and lit the kindling beneath it. Soon a roaring fire was engulfing the body of the sheep. Usually a feeling of optimism came from these ceremonies, but Ziba felt only a feeling of doom.

Just as King Saul stepped away from the fire, an old man in robe stepped forward.

"What do you think you're doing?" the man said. Ziba recognized Samuel, the prophet. Despite what appeared to be old age, the man carried himself with amazing authority and strength. Ziba stood in amazement at his audacity in talking to the king the way Samuel did.

In contrast, the kingly bearing of Saul disappeared. The tall, powerful man looked as if he'd just been caught stealing someone else's sheep. His head bowed, and when he spoke, the words came out in stutters.

"You didn't come. The men were scattering. I had to do something. I knew that eventually they'd even come after me here. I needed God's favor. You weren't here, so I did what kings are supposed to do. I took the initiative. I am king, after all."

"What you are is a fool," Samuel said, and the crowd gasped. Ziba watched the guards, waiting to see someone step forward to defend the king's honor, but no one did.

"God told you what to do, and you didn't do it. If you had, you and your sons would reign forever. You've shown that you won't obey God. You don't trust Him. Because of this, God will find someone who will trust Him and obey Him. A man after His own heart. And he'll be king."

Saul stared at Samuel, who looked at him, then simply shook his head and turned away.

"Wait," Saul said after Samuel. "Where are you going?"

"Gibeah," Samuel said. "There's nothing for me to do here."

The feeling of doom was as thick as heavy fog. Ziba watched the two men as they sadly separated from each other. Saul stood for a long moment staring at the departing Samuel, then at the fire that smoldered over the half-burned sheep. He looked lost.

Finally, Saul turned to see Abner coming toward him.

"Bad news," Abner said.

Saul didn't respond.

"No one else is coming," Abner said. "We just did a head count. We came with two thousand. We now have six hundred men."

Saul stared at him numbly, then nodded.

"Tell everyone to break camp," he said. "We're headed into battle."

Chapter 5

Once and Future King

A re you insane?" Abner nearly shouted back at the king of Israel on their way back to the tent. Jonathan and Ziba both were shocked with the tone that Abner used, one they had never heard anyone use with King Saul.

Abner must have realized how he sounded because he immediately caught himself.

"Forgive me, my king. But six hundred men, ill-equipped and many not even trained, attacking tens of thousands of professional, armored Philistines. To me that's madness."

Saul looked back at his general, torn between anger at Abner's rash tone and his own indecision. He said nothing for a long moment, looking first at Abner and then at Jonathan and Ziba. Ziba could see that Saul was struggling to decide whether to shout down his general or listen to his counsel. Finally he spoke, an edge in his voice.

"You tell me, Abner. Samuel, our spiritual leader, has abandoned us. Our men have abandoned us. Whether through cowardice or common sense, they've fled to their homes or perhaps the rocks and the caves to protect them from the Philistines. The land of Israel is completely open to the invading army. What am I supposed to do? What can six hundred men do?"

Jonathan spoke up from behind.

"Gideon won a great battle with just three hundred men," he said quietly. "If God is on our side, who can defeat us?"

See 1 Samuel 14.

"Is God on our side?" Saul muttered, mostly to himself. He stared out at his disappearing army. "I suspect that Jehovah has abandoned us."

"Perhaps we've abandoned Him," Jonathan continued. "Call for Samuel. Ask for forgiveness. Ask for God's direction. It's not too late, Father."

Ziba saw Abner stiffen. "A true king doesn't ask for forgiveness. A true king doesn't ask for the help of an old man."

Saul inhaled through his nose forcefully. "Abner is right. It's too late for Samuel. The people of Israel want to be led by a king, not by a prophet."

"So act like a king," Jonathan said. "Show them that any man, no matter how powerful, can ask for forgiveness. Set an example for them."

"No," Saul said quietly. "The people are watching me closely. They want to see strength, not weakness. I have to act." Saul stopped talking, and all watched him closely, realizing that he was thinking. The decision he made in the next few moments could decide the fate of all of them.

"We can't run and we aren't strong enough to attack," Saul said. He then turned toward Abner and motioned toward their map.

"If our forces aren't concentrated all in one place—and they definitely aren't—where will the Philistines go?"

Abner looked at the map for a long moment before responding.

"Their forces have been seen following the coast road north," he said. "If I were the Philistine commander, I'd want to put myself in a central location where I could send out raiding parties in all directions. At the same time, they'll want to camp in a spot that's easily defended." He looked for another long moment before shaking his head and pointing to the map.

"I still think it will be Michmash," he said. "It's across from the garrison at Geba. It controls the pass from east to west, and he can send raiders north, east, and west from there." He looked up. "If they're camped there in force, no general in his right mind would dare attack him."

Saul clenched his lips tightly and nodded. "It makes perfect sense. They'll take a strategic point in the middle of Israelite country and wait for us to attack. Well, we can't attack, but at least we can keep them from going south. We'll set up a blockade at the southern side of the pass." He pointed to Geba at the map.

"It's a good thing Jonathan took Geba," Ziba said helpfully.

Saul spun and faced the two of them, anger full on his face.

"If Jonathan had done what he was told to do, we wouldn't be in this mess. The Philistines would still be down on the plains where they belong. Instead, we'll be fighting them on our front steps. Do you consider that good, Ziba?"

Ziba shook his head. "No, Your Majesty."

Saul stared at Ziba for a long time before turning his gaze at Jonathan.

"However well-intentioned you were, Jonathan, you've sealed our fate. You may have killed us all."

"God won't let Israel fall," Jonathan said.

"Get out of here!" Saul shouted back at him, spittle flying from his lips. "Ziba, take Jonathan back to Gibeah. Don't let him out of your sight. From now on, crown prince, your duty is to stay in the palace and make sure I have an heir. I'll find you a wife as soon as possible, and you'll begin your most important duty of making babies. It has become obvious to me that's all you're good for."

Ziba watched Jonathan's face flush, and then he looked at the ground. Finally, Jonathan nodded and left the tent, his armor-bearer quietly following behind him.

It wasn't the first time that Mara had been to Gibeah. She still remembered her frantic ride seven years before when she called upon Saul to save her city. And on that day, after the Ammonites had been driven away, she remembered that her father had pledged her to serve in the king's court. It had been a gesture that shocked her at first, but over the years she'd begun to anticipate the day when she would return.

Seven years can mark a lot of changes, both for a city and for a young woman. At age sixteen, Mara was growing into a woman. And the city she now rode into, accompanied by her father, was growing as well. Gibeah was now the capital of Israel, and many workmen were combining their skills to convert it from a camp of tents into a proper city.

The center of it all was the royal palace. Stone walls were halfway completed, with the living quarters already finished and occupied. It wasn't as imposing as Gath, or for that matter Jabesh-gilead, but it wasn't finished either. With the palace as the center of the new city, Israelites were beginning to feel as though they could compete with other nations.

Mara wondered at the new palace as she rode alongside her father to its entrance. Two people waited at its steps. One she recognized as Michal, Jonathan's younger sister.

"Greetings," said the man with her. "We welcome you to Gibeah, the capital city of Israel. I am Hakesh, custodian for the royal court. I'm here to make sure you're settled and comfortable."

Mara's father got off his donkey first and then helped Mara off her donkey to the ground. Her father had bought her a new dress to wear to court, and she tried to look as ladylike as possible. But as she locked eyes with the younger Michal, whom she'd grown fond of on her trip seven years earlier, they both fought back a giggle.

"I'm Jabek, chief elder of Jabesh-gilead," her father said formally. "I'm here to escort my daughter to her new home. This is Mara."

"Welcome, Mara," said Hakesh, just as formally. "You'll be the assistant to Princess Michal. I believe you've already met her."

Once again, the two girls stifled a laugh. Then Michal spoke.

"Hakesh, I know you have lots to discuss with Mara's father. I'll take Mara to her quarters, then show her around the palace."

Hakesh cleared his throat and said, "Very well, Princess. I'll leave her in your care."

But the two girls had already left.

Jonathan and Ziba left for Gibeah right away, and within a day, what was left of Saul's army arrived as well. No one in the palace spoke of what faced them just north of Geba, but the rumors continued to fly through all of Gibeah. Ziba heard the palace staff tell of the massive Philistine army camped just north of the stockade they'd liberated, and of raiding parties that would steal, burn, and kill in all directions. Israelites had left their homes to hide in ravines, caves, and the forest of Ephraim, afraid for their lives with the armored might of the Philistines camped in their midst.

Not only was Jonathan confined to the palace in Gibeah; whenever he left his room he was followed by Ziba, as well as two more guards—soldiers Ziba knew were loyal to Saul above all. So rather than parading around the palace with an armored entourage, Jonathan chose to stay in his quarters.

After a week of this, both Ziba and Jonathan grew bored with the routine. Jonathan never saw his father and assumed that he was busy with organizing his forces against the Philistine threat.

"I've never been more bored in my life," Jonathan said finally, sitting on a stool at the foot of his bed. He played with a dagger that he'd received on his last birthday.

"Hey, try sheepherding," Ziba said, sitting in the window, looking out into the courtyard. "This is nothing." He watched two young women talking as they neared the palace. "Hello, ladies," he said loudly, waving.

The two girls giggled and hid their faces before one of them waved back at Ziba. Jonathan stood and looked over Ziba's shoulder.

"Who's that with Michal?" Jonathan asked. "I don't think I've seen her before."

"You have," Ziba corrected him. "It's just that it's been seven years, and a young woman can change a lot in that time. That's Mara from Jabesh-gilead. Remember her?"

Jonathan's eyebrow rose. "Oh, you mean the one with the—?" He tapped his finger at his eye, and Ziba nodded.

"Yeah, she looks pretty good now that she's found a better way of keeping it covered," Ziba said. As if she'd heard him, she looked up at the two young men, showing them a golden patch that she wore over the missing eye.

"It doesn't take long to forget that it's even there," Ziba said.

"Some lucky man will get her soon enough," Jonathan said. "How about you?"

Ziba shook his head. "You know I have eyes for only one girl."

Jonathan sighed. "And I told you, that's not going to happen. Michal is a princess; you're a—"

"Yeah, I know, I'm a servant. Just the hired help."

"I was going to say, you're the armor-bearer to the crown prince. Not a servant. But you're not royalty."

"All I know is that I've loved that girl since we were playing in the dust together. And the years have been very, very kind to her."

"Yeah, that's my sister you're talking about here," Jonathan said. "She may be pretty, but she knows it too. She plans on capitalizing on it, marrying some king or wealthy merchant, I suspect. You need a woman who's a better fit for who you are. Someone whom you won't have to take care of hand and foot."

"But I like her hands and feet very much," Ziba said, grinning.

"Enough of this talk about girls," Jonathan said. "I don't even want to think about who my father will arrange for me to marry. Let's talk about something more exciting."

"Like?"

"How about the Philistines?"

Ziba sighed and shook his head. "I'm tired of rehashing rumors."

"Who said anything about rumors? Let's go see for ourselves."

"Are you crazy? Your father will—"

"Will what? He already confined me to the palace. I'm the heir to the throne; he can't kill me. At least I don't think he will."

"But what about me? I'm no crown prince."

"What were his orders to you? Back in the tent at Gilgal. Do you remember? I do. He said, 'Don't let him out of your sight.' Didn't he?"

Ziba shrugged. "Yeah. So?"

"So how are you going to keep me in sight if I leave here? Such as for a little first-person view of the camp at Michmash?"

"He'll kill me! Jonathan, no."

"Look," Jonathan said, pointing out the window. "We wait for dark. We drop out the window—"

"That must be fifteen feet!"

"I figure twelve. Anyway, it's soft ground. It'll break your fall. Then we follow the wall over to the stables and take two fast horses. We'll be back before dawn."

Ziba looked skeptically at his companion.

"Whatever you do, I'm with you. Through thick or thin—" Jonathan looked at his companion hopefully, and Ziba finally nodded in agreement.

Ziba and Jonathan had ridden the road from Gibeah to Geba countless times, and they crossed the short distance, even in the dark, in less than an hour. Ziba was relieved to discover that the commander of the outpost at Geba was still their old friend, Uthai. The older man seemed surprised that Ziba and Jonathan had joined them at the compound, but covered it up quickly.

"We decided to come to take a look for ourselves," Jonathan said quickly. Uthai looked at Jonathan and then at Ziba, and nodded, a knowing look on his face.

"Don't worry, Uthai," Ziba said. "The prince has assured me that we'll be back in the palace by dawn."

"I require all of my soldiers here to be armed," Uthai said, gesturing to a stack of swords, spears, and shields that Ziba recognized from the attack on the Philistine garrison a week before. Ziba grabbed a sword and scabbard and handed it to Jonathan then also picked up a spear and shield.

Jonathan stepped past Uthai and walked to the edge of the cliff overlooking the ravine. Where a week ago, the cliffs on the other side had been dark, tonight they were alight with a hundred campfires. Jonathan looked at the few men he'd left there and noticed that quite a few campfires were burning on their side of the ravine as well.

"Better for the enemy to think there are more of us than there are," Uthai said. "Heaven knows that there's not much keeping them on their side as it is."

"What's keeping them over there?" Ziba asked. "They have to know they outnumber us twenty to one."

Uthai shook his head. "They want us to attack them. They've got a secure position, and they know their chariots won't do very well over here in the hills. So they raid and kill and plunder until we get sick of it and attack."

Jonathan shook his head. "Sooner or later, they're going to come right through this pass and down this road. It's just a matter of time."

"So what do we do?" Ziba asked. As the words left his mouth, he regretted saying them.

But Jonathan didn't respond. Instead, he patted Uthai on the shoulder and turned away.

"Thanks, Uthai. Time for us to head back."

Ziba breathed a sigh of relief as they went for their horses. But instead of mounting his horse, Jonathan grabbed the reins of his horse and led it east along the cliff facing the ravine. Ziba followed him silently, suspecting that Jonathan wanted a different view of the Philistine camp. They stopped at the last campfire that the Israelite soldiers maintained, and Jonathan spoke to the man there.

"There hasn't been much activity this way, other than taunts and comments about the deserters who are hiding in the hills," the soldier said. "I'm content for them to stay over there, and we'll stay over here."

"The trouble is, they won't stay over there forever," Jonathan said. Jonathan handed the reins of his horse over to the soldier and headed for the edge of the cliff. Before Ziba could stop him, Jonathan had started climbing down the cliff. Ziba quickly handed his reins over to the soldier as well and headed after him. Jonathan was at the bottom of the ravine before Ziba could catch up with him.

"What are you doing?" Ziba hissed at him, afraid to raise his voice too much. "This isn't a scouting expedition!"

Jonathan said nothing but kept creeping forward behind boulders toward the other side. Ziba could see the fires of the Philistines far above them.

"Remember when you and I found that big cypress tree and Father told us not to climb it?" Jonathan said. "And I bet you a week's allowance that you couldn't climb it blindfolded?"

Ziba nodded. "Yeah. So?"

"I can't imagine climbing this cliff in the dark could be any more difficult."

"What? Jonathan, no."

"They're going to attack us, or if we don't do something, they'll destroy the kingdom one town at a time. I won't wait any longer. Look."

Jonathan grabbed Ziba by the arm. "Are we God's people or not? Do you believe God will take care of you?"

Ziba bit his lip. "I believe God's angels protect me, but I don't want to go places God doesn't want me to go. How do you know this is God's will?"

Jonathan looked down and then nodded to himself. "OK, here's what we'll do. We'll come out and show ourselves to the Philistines. If they tell us to wait here, we'll wait and fight whoever comes down to us. If they say come up, we'll take that as a sign that God is with us and that's what He wants us to do. If we believe God is with us, nothing can stop us. Are you with me?"

Ziba looked long and hard at his companion, but he already knew the answer.

"Jonathan, a long time ago, I committed my fate to yours. I'm with you heart and soul. If we die here, so be it, but let's do it together."

Jonathan looked at his friend, slapped him on the shoulder, and nodded. Then he stood up, and Ziba followed him. A long minute later, they heard a voice from above speaking to them in broken Hebrew.

"Halloo down there," the voice said. Ziba saw a burly soldier in armor standing at the edge of the cliff. "Are you Israelites?"

"We are," Jonathan said.

"We thought all of the Israelites were still hiding in the caves." Ziba heard others laughing and could tell that they had been drinking. "We have plenty of wine here if you want to come join us. We even have some of your countrymen who are now in our army."

"If we come up there, it'll be only to fight and kill you," Jonathan said.

The Philistine laughed. "Well, then, come on up. It's really boring up here. Maybe you can liven things up, puny as you are."

Jonathan looked at Ziba, who nodded.

"We'll be right up," Jonathan shouted back.

Chapter 6

Two Men Against a Nation

T he thing you have to understand about the Philistine psyche is this," King Achish said through slurred speech, the golden goblet sloshing red wine on his regal robes. "Israel may have their God, but we have something even more impressive."

"And what's that, Mighty King?" Zephan said. She was trying her best to serve as a hostess in her modest home in Endor while the king of the most powerful nation in the region was entertained and a company of his armored guards stood outside.

"Guile." The word came out bluntly, and Zephan wasn't sure she'd heard it correctly. But then he continued.

"Israel has only one thing going for them, and that's been spotty at best. They want to be like everyone else and only remember their God when they realize how weak they really are. And so they go, back and forth, back and forth. They have the one thing.

"But the Philistine psyche consists of plans within plans within plans. We—*I*—know how the world works. It works through strong men, powerful men, intelligent men."

"Like Your Majesty."

"Exactly." His words began to slur again, and Zephan knew that the evening was drawing to a close, whether he had the wits to call it a night and retreat back to his camp or he fell asleep on her couch, floor—or bed.

"We've already won this war," Achish continued. "We outnumber

See 1 Samuel 14.

the Israelite army twenty to one, and we have armor and chariots and weapons that they don't have. One of our commanders has more combat experience than all of theirs combined. We have the strategic location. We're on higher ground."

Why is he telling me this? Zephan asked herself. *Could it be that with all of his advantages, he still has his doubts?*

"And even if we lose this battle, the war isn't over. Plans within plans within plans . . ." His voice began trailing off, and Zephan realized the time had come for him to leave. She stood and went swiftly to her door, calling the captain outside to take him back to his camp. Two men came in and half-carried the drunken king out to his horse.

Plans within plans. *Am I a part of his plans?* Zephan wondered as the soldiers rode away with their king.

Jonathan took the lead in their climb up the cliff in the dark. Ziba followed close behind, but he was having a hard time dodging all of the rocks and dirt that fell as Jonathan climbed above him.

"Watch it!" Ziba hissed as a particularly large rock came loose and hit him in the shoulder.

"Sorry," Jonathan said quietly. "We need to be quiet."

"Why?" Ziba hissed back. "Don't they know we're coming?"

Jonathan didn't answer, but they tried to be quiet anyway. On the one hand, Ziba wished they had a full moon that would light their way up the rocky cliff. On the other hand, he was grateful for the darkness. Even if the Philistines had invited them to come up, he had to admit that if the roles were reversed, he wouldn't expect the enemy to climb such a treacherous cliff in total darkness.

The minutes stretched into an hour. Ziba felt his arms, legs, and back straining, his eyes and hair were full of dirt and debris, and he struggled to keep from coughing because of the dust. Finally he saw Jonathan disappear above him, and he realized that they'd reached the lip of the cliff. He continued climbing for another minute, then saw a hand reach down to pull him up. He took it and joined Jonathan on the top.

They both sat on the grassy top of the cliff, looking at each other in silence. While they gathered their breath, Ziba looked around them. The place where they sat was slightly lower than the rest of the plateau where the camp was situated. The sounds of revelry from earlier had died down, and, apparently, most of the camp had gone to sleep. Ziba raised himself up cautiously and looked closer.

"They don't even have a guard up at this point," Ziba said in amazement. "We could walk all the way to the other side of the camp, and no one would ever know."

"Our business isn't at the other side of the camp," Jonathan said quietly. Ziba watched in amazement as Jonathan stood up and pulled out his sword. "Watch my back."

"Always." Ziba stood and pulled out his spear and loosened up the shield that he'd carried up on his back.

Jonathan stepped forward quickly and came over the rise onto the plateau. A small fire had burned down to embers, and Ziba saw that the man who had talked to them what seemed like an eternity before was sitting hunched over by the fire. Ziba watched as Jonathan took his sword and put the blade beneath the chin of the sleeping man. A scowl came over the man's face as he lifted his chin and opened his eyes. When he saw the two Israelites standing before him, his face took on a look of surprise.

"Knock, knock," Jonathan said, then ran the blade over the man's throat. The man's eyes rolled back in his head, his hands clutched his throat, and his legs began to kick the fire.

The kicking legs stirred two others who lay near the fire, and Ziba wasted no time. He rammed the spear into the neck of one and the chest of the other.

"We need to be quieter, or this whole camp will wake up," Ziba said.

"Well, they're bound to wake up sooner or later," Jonathan said, running his sword through another sleeping Philistine.

"Let's make sure as many as possible never wake up again," Ziba said. He jabbed another sleeping Philistine with his spear, but this one screamed.

"I guess naptime is over," Ziba remarked.

With the scream, most of the men kept sleeping, but one or two raised their heads. One, apparently an officer, actually stood up and began to shout.

"To arms! To arms! The enemy is among us!"

At that, many more began to stand up. Many of the men had stripped their armor from themselves, and most were unarmed. Jonathan and Ziba kept stabbing, hacking, and spearing as many men as they could. But within a minute or two, they found Philistine soldiers, some armored and some not, surrounding them.

"At last!" Jonathan shouted. "Someone to fight!"

Ziba could see that most of them were still hung over from the previous night. As Jonathan waded deeper into the camp, swinging and stabbing as he went, Ziba followed him. One or two tried to get around Jonathan and attack them from the rear, but every time someone jumped forward, Ziba stuck them through the chest or stomach with his spear.

Time seemed to stand still as Ziba and Jonathan became surrounded by more and more Philistines. It wasn't until the sun rose in the east, blood red over the hillside, that Ziba realized they'd been there for several hours.

The red sunrise shone down on what looked like a nightmare of hell. The reddish light showed a camp littered with the dead and dying, blood spattered against tents and bedrolls, some tents on fire, and panic all around them. And in the middle of it stood two men who looked like demons, faces blackened by soot and dust, swinging and stabbing as if sent by their God to dispatch as many of the Philistines as possible to their version of the afterlife.

That's what Ziba saw. In their drunken stupor, the Philistines saw much worse. The panic was on the edge of being out of control when one Philistine captain stood above the others, spear in hand.

"Look at them! Look at them! There are only two of them! Take them!" he shouted. His words made sense to the Philistines, and Ziba realized that the battle was about to turn against them.

"Oh mighty God," he breathed, even as he continued fighting.

A moment later, he felt God's reply. His gut began churning, and suddenly he felt as if he were in a boat on a lake. The ground rose and fell around him. A second later, there was a roar like a waterfall, and the ground became like water. The Philistine captain who had stood so bravely and tried to rally the troops fell, and a horse began to trample him into the dirt. And Ziba saw that the battle was no longer in their hands.

This was God's battle.

"What's going on?" King Saul said as he entered the command tent outside Gibeah. He'd bivouacked his six hundred troops outside the town and joined them, mostly to make sure that they didn't abandon him as well.

"We're getting scattered reports that something is happening in the Philistine camp," Abner said, his face glued to the map laid out before them.

"Are they mustering for an attack?" Saul asked.

"I don't know," Abner said.

"Well, find someone who *does* know," Saul said. "This could be it." The unspoken words that both of them thought were *This could be the end.*

As they spoke, they heard the sound of a horse galloping toward them. A few seconds later, an out-of-breath soldier pulled the flap away and started to rush into the tent. The two armed guards there stopped him, but Saul waved them away.

"It's all right," Saul said. "You're one of Uthai's men, aren't you?"

"Yes, Your Majesty. Amnen, sir."

"Well, spit it out. What do you have for me?"

"Commander Uthai says that fighting has broken out in the Philistine camp," Amnen said.

"Fighting? Could it be just a brawl?"

"No, Your Majesty. It's happening near the Geba garrison. Our scouts say they can see dead bodies, many of them. One of the attackers is using a spear, and the other is using a sword."

"Could it be Edomites? Ammonites?" Saul said.

"No, I don't think so. That sounds like Israelites," Abner said.

"And there were only two?"

Amnen nodded. "That we saw. But there were so many bodies, there have to be many more attackers. But that's not what's so significant."

"What's so significant?"

"The entire camp is in a panic. They were shouting so loud we could hear it in Geba."

Saul looked at Abner.

"This is our sign. Either we take this opportunity or we give it all up."

"But, Your Majesty," Abner said, "they still outnumber us."

Saul opened his mouth to respond, but he never got the words out. The ground rolled beneath them in the morning light, and both of them fell to the floor. Saul jumped back up as soon as he could, his face flushed with excitement.

"God hasn't forgotten us!" he nearly shouted. "If that's not a sign, I don't know what is. Muster the troops. Find out who's missing. I'd wager my teeth that those two men are Israelites. They're brave men, and we won't leave them there to die."

"But, Your Majesty," Abner stammered, "how can we think of attacking when they outnumber us twenty to one?"

"How outnumbered are those two? And what stopped them? Are you and I lesser men than they?"

Another horse was heard, riding hard. This time, Saul didn't wait for the messenger to come inside the tent but opened the flap and went out to meet him.

"Look at that sky, Abner! God has given us another sign. The sky may be red, but it's not as red as the ground where those Philistines are camped. We'll meet them, and we'll defeat them."

The horseman had handed his reins to another man and now bowed before the king.

"Your Majesty," he said, then hesitated.

"Speak up, son," Saul said. "Do you have more good news for me?"

The young man looked up at the king for a long moment before speaking.

"Your Majesty, the crown prince Jonathan and his armor-bearer are missing."

Saul looked at the young man, then at Abner, and his lips drew back into a thin line. Somehow, it all now made sense.

❧

The sun rose higher in the sky, and it beat down on the two of them, but Ziba didn't dare pause to wipe the sweat from his eyes. Even after the shock of the earthquake, the number of Philistines around them had grown so thick that all he could see were armored Philistines. The battered bronze shield he carried, a relic from their night attack on the Geba garrison, grew heavier with each moment. He jabbed time and again around him at the hesitant Philistines, who were more concerned with keeping Jonathan and him cut off than in killing them.

Jonathan was behind him, his sword swinging and jabbing with an erratic rhythm, and even though he dared not look at him, Ziba could tell that he was getting tired as well. It was only a matter of time.

"Funny," Ziba said to Jonathan over his shoulder. "I never pictured us dying this way. Together, back to back, in battle. I'm not complaining, mind you. It's just that—" He paused to skewer another Philistine.

"Just that what?"

"I always imagined I'd die surrounded by my grandchildren."

Ziba heard Jonathan laugh behind him.

"You're much too young to be thinking about grandchildren. First, you need a wife."

"Yeah, well, we've already had that discussion. You know how I feel about that." Ziba heard Jonathan hack at another Philistine, followed by a howl.

"Well, I'm not letting you marry my sister," Jonathan said. "She's not right for you." Jab. Smack with the shield. Swipe. Scream.

"At this point, it all seems pretty moot," said Ziba. "I don't see a way out of this for us."

"God got us here," Jonathan said. "God will get us out."

I pray so, Ziba said to himself and continued fighting. *God, get us out of here.*

A few minutes later, he noticed that the number of Philistines on the side opposite the cliff was getting smaller, and then he saw them turn and begin fighting someone else.

"Jonathan!" he shouted.

"I see," Jonathan said. "They're fighting each other. Wait. Those are Israelites!"

Ziba watched with one eye as he continued fighting and saw that the Philistines were fighting other troops. They were dressed like Philistines, but their hair was long instead of cropped short in the Philistine style, and their physical features were different. A few minutes later, Ziba and Jonathan were facing only three men. Half a minute later, they were alone, surrounded by dead Philistines.

"Where are they going?" Ziba asked.

"Look," Jonathan said. A dozen men broke away from the sides that were fighting each other and ran toward them. Ziba raised his spear and shield to defend them, but Jonathan put his hand out, and Ziba lowered them.

The men stopped a few feet away from the two and immediately dropped to their knees, bowing their heads.

"Your Highness," one said. "I'm Mareshah of the tribe of Judah."

"Get up, you idiot," Ziba said to him, taking the free moment to wipe his face with a rag. "You want the whole world to know that the crown prince of Israel is in the middle of the Philistine camp?"

The men rose quickly.

"Mareshah, what are you doing here?" Jonathan asked.

Mareshah and the others hung their heads. "We were among the hundreds who joined the Philistines. We didn't have the courage to fight what we considered overwhelming odds. But when we saw you, *you* and your companion, fighting when we wouldn't, taking on the entire army, we couldn't stand by and let it happen."

"How many are there of you?" Ziba asked.

"Not many," Mareshah said. "A few hundred."

"But that's a few hundred more than we had last night," Jonathan said. "And we're in the middle of them. With you dressed like that," Jonathan gestured at the Philistine armor the men wore, "the Philistines won't know who's their enemy and who's their friend."

"We're ready, Prince Jonathan," Mareshah said. "Just tell us what to do."

"The first thing you do is find us some horses," Jonathan said. "If this battle goes the way I think it will, the Philistines will be running soon. And I've no intention of letting them get away."

The army of Israel consisted of one thousand men—a few hundred guards from Gibeah had joined the six hundred bivouacked outside the city. Saul wished he had horses for all of them—to be truthful, he wished he had better weapons and training for all of them—but he had to go with what he had. Even now he felt a fire stirring in him, a fire he hadn't felt since he'd first hacked two oxen into twelve pieces years ago. And he recognized the fire for what it was.

Saul looked out at the motley group of Israelites, all who had heard the rumor of a battle going on north of them, and then looked up at the sun. It was mid morning, hours since he'd heard of the battle.

"We've run out of time, Abner," Saul said. "Reports tell us that the battle is growing hotter, and yet we're not a part of it. I have to lead our army into battle."

"Sir . . . Your Majesty . . . you can't be replaced," Abner said. "In all likelihood, it's your son in the battle, and he may have already been killed. We can't afford to lose you, too. Let me take the men on horses and attack. March the men as fast as you can and join us at Geba."

Saul looked at Abner, then at the sun, then at the troops. It was all madness anyway, and there was no hope of overcoming such massive numbers of Philistines. And yet, God had shown that he wasn't alone.

"No, Abner," he said finally. "God is calling me. I'll take the soldiers on horseback. You join us as soon as you can."

Abner watched in horror as Saul motioned for the horsemen to follow him and began to ride the eight miles north to Geba.

Chapter 7

The Oath

I t took about two hours for Abner to march the bulk of Israel's army the eight miles to Geba. When he arrived at noon, Saul had committed the garrison at Geba to an all-out frontal assault on the Philistines across the ravine.

Even from the other side, it was obvious that the commanders of the Philistines were having a hard time rallying their troops. The pervasive partying the night before and the surprise attack at dawn followed by the earthquake had been too much for many of the superstitious Philistines. Even though they worshiped Baal, Dagon, or another one of the many false gods common throughout Canaan, most of the Philistine soldiers were familiar with stories of the God of Israel, a God who was all too real when it came time to rescue Israel from the folly of their actions.

Clusters of Philistine soldiers fought on, gathered by hardened, courageous officers. But as Abner watched from the outpost at Geba, he realized that the Philistines were fighting a battle on two fronts—in many cases against an enemy that they couldn't recognize.

Abner took the luxury of five full minutes at Geba to catch his breath and see where he should commit his army. Then he turned back to his men.

"Soldiers of Israel," he shouted over the mass of volunteers before him. "Your crown prince is over there. Your king is over there. Will we let them fight this battle without us?"

See 1 Samuel 14.

As one, the crowd shouted, "No!"

"Then we will attack!" Abner said.

"General," one man interjected from the front row, "we're not cowards, but many of us don't have a weapon. How can we fight?"

"Those of you with weapons will lead the attack. The rest of you watch. When a Philistine falls—or even when one of your comrades falls—pick up their weapon. You may not have a weapon right now, but there'll be weapons soon."

And with a mighty roar, he led the mostly unarmed army of Israel into battle with their fiercest and most dangerous enemy.

"There's no need to panic," Achish said to his two generals. "I don't want fear to continue spreading through the camp. I don't need rumors, speculation, or hearsay. What I do need are good, solid reports." His head ached from the wine he'd drunk the night before. He looked at Nob, his general in charge of chariots, and then at Gerar, his infantry general. He'd been with the two of them long enough to sense that they were unnerved, which bothered him as well. *This situation is unraveling very quickly*, he thought. *I need to do something right now.*

"General Nob, what's the status of your chariots?"

"The chariots are in good shape at the east side of camp," Nob answered. "However, the horses are on the north side."

"How in Dagon's tail did that happen?" Achish said.

"Excuse me, Your Majesty, but we'd worn down the grazing land to the east, and we moved them so that they wouldn't starve."

"Wouldn't starve? Well, get them over to the east side!"

"Right away, Your Majesty, but there's fighting in between."

"Fighting? Who's fighting?"

"We're not exactly sure," said Gerar. "Reports are spotty."

"Spotty? *Spotty!* Get me some confirmed reports!" Achish found his voice rising and getting shrill, and he caught himself. It wouldn't work to let his generals think he'd lost all control. He took a minute and calmed his voice.

"Listen, do we or do we not still outnumber the Israelites?"

"We do, Your Majesty. Many times over," Nob replied.

"Do we or do we not have better armor, chariots, training, and weapons?"

"That's true, Your Majesty," agreed Nob.

"Are you two not the veterans of countless campaigns against Egypt, Moab, and a dozen other countries?"

Nob cleared his throat. "We are, Your Majesty."

Achish stared at both of them. "Then do your job. *Win this battle*."

Saul's riders attacked the Philistines without pause as soon as they arrived in Geba. Saul only took a minute to order Uthai to muster every man he could find and follow them into the pass and against the still-confused Philistines. Uthai blew the *shofar* the garrison kept for many purposes: two short blasts and then one long. It was the signal throughout Israel for an all-out attack. *Attack. Attack.* Without anyone saying so, the men who fought for Israel's side knew that they were not only fighting a common enemy and fighting for their king, they were fighting for their lives and the lives of their children. All had wanted to fight, but none had the courage to fight. Someone had found that courage. And now the battle was engaged, with the future of Israel at stake.

"Keep blowing it, Uthai," Saul said. "Every time you blow it, our troops know that we're still in the battle. Every time you blow, they know that I'm still here."

As he spoke, an arrow caught the soldier on his right in the chest, and he fell from his tall horse.

"Your Majesty," Uthai said. "The enemy is scattering before us, but we're too high to strike them. And there's the danger of an arrow striking you off your horse. We need to dismount."

"Very well," Saul said grudgingly. "Have two men take the horses toward the rear. But we have to press forward. If we pause, the Philistines will regroup, and it'll be a different battle altogether. We need to cut off their western flank."

"But then the enemy will get behind us and cut us off," Uthai objected.

"I don't want any Philistines escaping this battlefield!" Saul shouted, grabbing him by the collar. "We cut off the western flank, and we cut off their means of escape."

Saul gestured toward the west, and his men pushed forward as fast as they could, hacking and stabbing their way through the weak opposition.

The sun shone down unmercifully hot in the midday heat, and his men grew faint, but Saul was unrelenting. To him, the red dawn had covered his vision. He was in a battle haze, where all around him was tinted red. This battle was everything to him.

Then Saul heard the shofar behind him. He turned to Uthai, who fought next to him. "Abner has arrived with reinforcements." The Philistines they were fighting heard the sound of the horn as well, and Saul could see them sag visibly in their efforts. Then Saul heard another shofar, this one far off to his right. He looked at Uthai.

"That has to be the two men who started all this," Saul said. *Jonathan*, Saul thought.

Uthai stretched to see to the east. "If it's them, they've received reinforcements of their own." He pointed to the dust cloud that showed the battle line to the east.

"Outstanding!" Saul said. And then they heard another shofar, this one to the north.

Two short, one long. *Attack.*

"Your Majesty!" said the messenger, falling on his face before Achish. "Fresh forces have fallen on our soldiers to the north."

"Who are they?" Achish asked, an edge in his voice.

"We don't know, Your Majesty, but many believe that Israelites who were hiding in the caves of Ephraim heard of the battle and have come to join their brothers."

"*Then they'll die with their brothers!*" Achish shouted. He looked over at Nob and Gerar, who slowly shook their heads.

"What is it?" Achish spat, his control rapidly falling away.

"Your Majesty, this is one battle. If we leave now, we can regroup and fight again later," Gerar said.

"Why in Baal's belly would I do that?"

Nob stepped forward and pointed at the map.

"We are cut off from all exits north, east, and south. Our only way out is the way we came."

"Retreat?" Achish asked, his face turning white.

Gerar nodded quickly. "A *tactical* retreat, Your Majesty. Our troops are out of control, and we've been unsuccessful in restoring order. If we retreat now, we retain most of our strength and can attack again when the battle is more in our favor."

"And if we retreat now, Gath doesn't lose her king," Achish added, thinking to himself. He looked at Gerar, and then at Nob, then nodded slightly.

"Ready my chariot," he said. "I leave in fifteen minutes."

It took a while for the men to find horses for Jonathan and Ziba, enough for them and their small command. In the meantime, more and more Israelites who had joined the Philistines began turning back to Israel in defense of the crown prince. By the time that Mareshah had found a dozen horses, nearly a hundred men were fighting by the side of Jonathan and Ziba.

"We can't leave them here," Ziba said, once again wiping the sweat and blood from his forehead. He'd been nicked at the hairline about an hour before, and blood continued to run into his eyes. "We have to stay here and fight."

"We will, Ziba," Jonathan said. "It's not time to use the horses. When the panic starts, we'll need them. Remember, there are thousands of Philistine soldiers, but only one King Achish."

"And only one Prince Jonathan, remember that," Ziba added.

"Something I'm sure you won't let me forget," Jonathan replied, grinning.

They fought for another hour, pressing continually westward. They heard the sound of the shofar to the south.

"Father is here," Jonathan said.

"Will it be enough?" Ziba asked him.

"Now we're an army again!"

Ziba grinned, and Jonathan grinned back.

They heard the shofar blow again, then heard another farther to the south.

"Reinforcements," Ziba said to Jonathan. "This is getting better all the time."

Then they heard the blast from still another shofar, this one off to the north. They looked at each other.

"Who is that?" Ziba asked. Jonathan shrugged.

"Just keep pushing forward. We'll find out soon enough."

A few minutes later a shout came from among the Philistines, and then another. Then Ziba could see a panic striking them all. As one, the men they'd been fighting began to run away from them. They grabbed one Philistine soldier, dirty and half dressed, and held a sword at his throat.

"Why is everybody running?" Ziba asked.

"King Achish has fled the battlefield!" he said, his eyes as big as saucers. "Please don't kill me."

"Fight with us then," Jonathan said. "Help us kill this coward king of yours."

The man nodded. "I never liked him anyway."

The Israelite soldiers began to chase the fleeing Philistines, but Jonathan held up his hand, and they paused.

"We have a dozen horses. Ten of you come with Ziba and me. We're going after Achish. The rest of you go north and link up with whatever mystery force has joined our side up there. Mareshah, you're in charge."

Ziba and Jonathan mounted their horses, and ten joined them. Exhausted, bleeding, and without food or water for almost a day, the twelve of them headed west at a gallop.

"They're breaking! They're breaking!" Uthai said, his sword finding rest in the skull of another Philistine.

Saul looked over the crowd and saw what Uthai was talking about. Even with the many hundreds they'd killed, thousands of Philistines stood before them like an ocean. But it was a receding ocean. Saul could see that the soldiers in the distance were moving west, not toward them. And like the tide, the pull of the retreat took on a life of its own. Soon, only a few men stood before them, with the others in full flight.

"We can't let them escape!" Saul shouted. He looked behind him and saw that Abner and his infantry had joined them without his seeing it.

"But, Your Majesty," Abner urged, "our men are exhausted and starving. We didn't bring any food or water. Surely a ten-minute break to refresh ourselves won't make that much difference."

"Look at me," Saul said to Abner, and Abner could see the blood in his eyes. Then he raised his voice to those who gathered around him. "Look at me, all of you.

"This I swear before God. If any man stops for food before this day is over, I put a curse on them, and they are under sentence of death! I'll have my vengeance on my enemies! That's my oath!

"Now, onward!"

Jonathan, Ziba, and their followers hacked their way through the dense crowd of fleeing Philistines, pushing ever westward. Within minutes, the Israelite lines were left behind them, and they were completely surrounded by armored and half-armored Philistine soldiers.

But these were not the disciplined ranks that had frightened everyone in Israel for so long. Many had already dropped their armor and weapons and were scrambling and jostling past one another in a desperate attempt to run from the battlefield.

"Look at them run!" Ziba said. "It's almost a shame to cut them down." He paused. "Almost."

"Over that rise is the village of Beth-aven," said Jonathan, pointing ahead of them with his bloody sword. "Beyond that is Aijalon. If the king gets that far, we've lost him. It's open country on the other side, and we'll never catch him."

"How fast can a Philistine chariot go?" Ziba asked, and Jonathan looked at him. Ziba grinned. "It depends on how many Israelites are chasing it."

Jonathan grinned back. "Well, let's hope we're faster than Achish's chariot today."

"Hyah!" Ziba yelled and kicked his horse, and the others followed suit. They continued to push westward through the densely packed crowd of fleeing men.

The sun was setting by the time Saul, Abner, and the rest of the Israelite army got to Aijalon. They were wounded, tired, hot, thirsty, and hungry after an entire day of battle, but Saul had been unrelenting. Behind them lay a solid path of bodies—Philistine soldiers who hadn't been fast enough to escape the wrath of Saul and his newly weaponized Israelite army.

Saul rode next to Abner through the town, their frantic first efforts having given way to a steady trot. Horses and men were exhausted; it was obvious to everyone there. But Saul still had blood in his eye and a fixed, almost insane look on his face. He and Abner kept riding west until they reached the far end of the town. There they met Jonathan and Ziba, surrounded by their ten companions.

Ziba had found a barrel of water and was washing the blood from his scalp and face. Red water ran like rivers down his leather armor. Around him, the other men sat propped against a stone wall, many of them drinking water from the same barrel.

Jonathan sat on the steps of a nearby house, watching his father approach as he ate honey.

"If you're looking for Achish, you're too late," he said to his father casually. "He and his royal guard came through here about an hour ago."

"When did you get here?" Saul asked, an edge in his voice.

"About ten minutes too late," Jonathan said.

After arriving in Aijalon, Saul inquired of the Lord about pursuing the Philistines. When God did not answer him, Saul called together the leaders to discover who had sinned that day. The lot fell on Jonathan.

"Jonathan, what did you eat today? Didn't you hear my oath?"

"No, Father, I didn't hear your oath," Jonathan said, suddenly very serious.

Saul sighed, and Abner cleared his throat.

"Your Majesty, your word is law," he said. "Once you've made a command, it has to be carried out."

Saul looked at his son, then at the men around Jonathan, then turned to the men behind him.

"Abner's right," Saul said sadly. "I've made an oath. No one can break a blood oath and live. Jonathan has to die."

Ziba stepped between Jonathan and Saul.

"Over my dead body," he hissed, lifting his spear in front of him threateningly. The others who had ridden with Jonathan stepped forward and joined Ziba in front of Jonathan, many of them drawing their swords.

"Your Majesty!" Saul heard behind him. He turned, and a battle-scarred Uthai stood with the rest of the army. "Your son has won a great battle today. If it weren't for him, we'd still be huddled in our homes, wondering when the Philistines would come to take them away from us. Instead, we've driven them from our land."

A cheer went up from behind Uthai. Then someone started a chant, and others quickly joined him.

"*Jonathan! Jonathan! Jonathan!*"

Saul sat on his horse and looked at the men who had followed him into battle against overwhelming odds, then at Abner, who had helped him lead those men, then at Uthai, then at Ziba and his comrades, then at his son Jonathan. The chanting went on, louder and louder for several minutes.

"*Jonathan! Jonathan! Jonathan!*"

Finally Saul held up his hand for silence.

"I've sworn a blood oath. My word is law. What can I do?"

"Free him!" shouted someone, and others quickly joined in.

"*Free him! Free him! Free him!*"

Uthai stepped forward, and the other men stopped chanting.

"Your Majesty," said Uthai. "I've heard your blood oath. But this man—your son—was used by God today. What he did today was

God's doing. What are you saying to God if your word is more important to you than God's doing? I swear not a hair shall fall from Jonathan's head today."

Uthai walked slowly around Saul's horse and stood with Ziba in front of Jonathan. Others began to join him until there were more in front of Saul than there were behind him.

"Very well," Saul said, looking in amazement at the crowd before him. "I'll agree that God has used Jonathan to create a miracle today. But he's still broken my oath. Because of this, I'll no longer take him into battle with me. Jonathan will be relieved of his command from this day forward. He'll remain at the palace.

"He has two brothers," Saul continued. "Maybe they'll be more willing to obey orders than their older brother is."

Ziba looked at Saul, then at Jonathan. *If Jonathan is removed from command, he won't need an armor-bearer. What will happen to me?*

Chapter 8

To the Last Man

L et me see if I understand you correctly," King Agag of Amalek said over his plateful of mutton, a glass of wine in his hand. "You—King Achish, lord over the powerful Philistines and the mightiest army in the Fertile Crescent—want me to attack the Israelites? Where are *your* soldiers? *Your* chariots? You want *me* to do the thing that lost you your army?"

Achish cleared his throat, and the music playing from the corner stopped. He turned and looked at his master guard, who nodded and ushered the musicians, entertainers, and servers out of the room. When Achish was alone with Agag, the king of Philistia turned to his guest.

"In essence, yes," he said calmly. "Even though I haven't lost my army, our forces have been badly damaged. We need time to regroup, to retrain new soldiers, to make new chariots, to purchase new horses. You can buy us that time."

Agag chuckled and put his wine goblet down on the table.

"Of course we could," he said. "But at what cost? We have no squabble with the Israelites, at least right now. We learn by watching other nations in their dealings with Israel. And what I see is this: *let sleeping dogs lie.*"

Achish leaned forward. "I could make it worth your while."

Agag snorted. "No, you couldn't. There isn't anything you have that we want."

See 1 Samuel 15

Achish paused. "Not even your own seaport? And perhaps a dozen ships to get started?"

Agag hesitated. Sea trading had made the Philistines powerful, and Amalek had always envied them for it. It was a tempting offer. But . . .

"No," Agag said, shaking his head and standing suddenly. "I'm too old and too smart to fall for your bribery. Attacking Israel right now, while they have their dander up, would be suicide. I'd rather be a poor nation than a former nation."

Achish bit his lip and opened his mouth to speak, but Agag waved him down.

"Achish, old friend, begging doesn't suit you, so don't start now. Philistia will have to deal with its own problems. It's time for me to go home."

Achish watched as Agag left the room, knowing that his entourage would join him as soon as he exited the building. By tomorrow, they'd be back in their own homes.

"That didn't turn out the way you expected," came a woman's voice from a dark corner. Zephan leaned forward, and Achish saw her shapely form.

"No. No, it didn't." He stared at the dark entrance as if trying to follow Agag into the night, and Zephan let him sit in silence.

"You've been coming here for quite a while now," Achish said, still not looking in Zephan's direction.

"Yes, Your Majesty. Seven years."

"And are your lessons meeting your expectations?" He turned slowly toward her and smiled slightly.

She nodded, reaching out her right hand in front of her. She opened the palm and blew. Blue flames flew forward from her breath into the air in front of her, lighting up her dark corner. Achish nodded in approval.

"Impressive," he said.

"I have a lot to be grateful for, my king," she said.

Zephan stood and walked out of the dark corner, her movements very much like a snake.

"I have a task for your son."

Zephan smiled broadly. "We live to serve."

It was the largest gathering that Gibeah and the new palace had ever seen. It was definitely the biggest festival that Ziba had ever seen. Israelites from north and south had gathered for the wedding of Jonathan to Rahab, daughter of Hirt, leader of the tribe of Ephraim.

It had been three months since the Battle of Michmash, and Jonathan was still seen as a hero, even overshadowing the king in the eyes of many of the younger Israelites. The victory at Michmash and the apparent destruction of the Philistine army had turned the timid into the brave, the quiet into the boastful, the shepherd into the soldier.

While Abner was busy equipping and training the massive army that had resulted from their victory, Saul was committed to bonding the Israelites in the north to those in the south. His answer to this challenge was the marriage that faced Jonathan today. It was purely a marriage of political expediency, and everyone knew it. Saul needed to make the northern tribes feel more a part of the new kingdom, and Jonathan needed an heir as well. But the fact that the marriage was necessary didn't stop the people from celebrating.

The walls of the new capital were still under construction, and even though the palace was completed, Jonathan had requested that the ceremony take place in the garden outside so that more people could witness the event. The morning was beautiful, the sun was shining, and Jonathan stood across from his bride. Much to his chagrin, Jonathan had been dressed in finery by palace servants, his armor and sword put away in exchange for rich robes of gold and red. Facing him was his soon-to-be bride, veiled and unrecognizable under her version of wedding attire. It was as if Jonathan were marrying a large mound of delicate cloth, with only her hand visible to the public and her future husband.

The two of them stood in front of Samuel, who had left his home in Ramah to officiate at the wedding of the crown prince of Israel. Samuel looked the same, regardless of the occasion: white and brown robes, his walking stick never too far away. The conflict between Saul and Samuel at Gilgal was for the moment forgotten, and the focus was on the young couple—the future king and queen of Israel.

"God has called for me to do many things, and one of the most enjoyable is to unite these two young people . . ."

Sitting in his favorite window in Jonathan's room overlooking the wedding, Ziba heard Samuel's voice echo from under the marriage canopy to carry across the tide of people. Jonathan had requested that Ziba accompany him onto the platform as his second, but he'd been overruled. Jonathan and Ziba had discovered early on that because the event was a national occasion, Jonathan and his new bride had very little say in what happened.

It's just as well, Ziba thought, watching the ceremony from the window. *No one else has the view I have.* His eyes scanned the crowd of people assembled to see one particular person.

"You can't see her from here," a voice came from behind him. He turned to see Mara, dressed in a blue silken robe with an eye patch to match. He'd seen her only from a distance since she'd arrived; now that they were closer, he realized just how much she'd grown up. He thought back to the gawky, heroic girl who had saved her entire city from the Ammonites. The woman standing before him now didn't look gawky at all.

"She's standing with her sister, Merab, under the entryway," Mara said, a slight smile on her lips. "They didn't want to get too much sun."

"It's not that hot out there," Ziba said, suddenly confused.

"I know," Mara said. "But they're less interested in the temperature and more concerned with whether the sun would make them look too brown." Her faint smile grew larger, and Ziba realized that he liked her smile.

"What are you doing in here, then?" Ziba asked.

"A wedding is wonderful to watch, but there's still work to do. Someone has to prepare the tables for the feast afterward."

"We have servants for that," Ziba said. "You're Michal's attendant. Surely they can spare you to see the wedding."

"We?" Mara said, laughing. "You act as if you're not a servant. As if you're one of them."

Ziba's face reddened. Mara was right; he'd worked and fought so closely with Jonathan that he'd forgotten that in essence he was what his father was and always had been: a servant. But no . . .

"I'm the armor-bearer and bodyguard to the crown prince," Ziba said. "I'm no mere servant."

Mara covered her mouth, but Ziba could see that her grin was still there.

"And do your duties include protecting him on his wedding night?"

Ziba's face reddened again, and he looked down.

"I hope you're enjoying yourself, making fun of me," Ziba said.

Mara grew more serious, still a small smile on her lips.

"Do you remember me? I remember you."

Ziba looked up. "Of course I do. You're the girl who saved her entire city."

"And lost an eye," Mara added. "And you're the boy who made friends with me around the campfire in Bezek. Those were simpler times."

"Simpler? I'd think they were pretty much the same as now. Surrounded by enemies. Every day the danger of being attacked from any direction."

"Well, at least we have a day to celebrate," Mara said, looking down at the couple surrounded by a friendly crowd. "It's a beautiful day outside, and we should take advantage of it."

Ziba watched the young woman, admiring not only her beauty but the innate courage that he realized still existed in her. Then he shook himself mentally and turned his thoughts back to Michal.

Ziba was thinking about their conversation an hour later while seated at the large table for the wedding feast. Ziba was seated quite a distance away from the main table. While a larger gathering was assembled outside, which had grown to nearly a thousand, the gathering inside was by invitation only. At the main table, in addition to the wedding couple, sat the prophet Samuel; Saul and his wife, Ahinoam; Jonathan's older sister, Merab; his younger sister, Michal; and his younger brothers, Ishvi,* Malki-Shua, and little Eshbaal.† Abner, general of the army

---

* Also called Abinadab.

† Later known as Ishbosheth.

of Israel, stood in the corner nearby.

Ziba was not part of the royal family, yet his actions at the Battle of Michmash and his closeness to Jonathan justified his being included as part of the main wedding party. Although Michal was seated at the end of the main table, Ziba saw Mara only when she came in and out as she helped the servants who waited on tables.

Saul had decided that the feast would celebrate their victory over the Philistines as well as the wedding, and so it was the largest gathering that they had been at, with the exception of a few battles. Ziba preferred this kind of gathering, although as he looked at Jonathan seated next to his bride, her face still completely covered, he felt a degree of sympathy for him. Even though others told of Rahab's beauty, Ziba wondered if he could marry someone he wouldn't see face-to-face until the wedding night.

Musicians had been playing for most of the feast, and men and then young women had gotten up to dance. Ziba watched the older men get up to dance, and one had invited him to join them, but he'd refused, knowing that he was much more talented with a spear and shield than he was on the dance floor.

When the young women got up to dance, Ziba paid a great deal more attention. On the second song, Ziba saw Michal gesture to Mara, who stood in the corner of the room. They giggled to each other as they joined the women dancing on the floor. Ziba watched the two of them, and after a long moment realized that he was having a difficult time deciding which one he preferred to watch. But as he watched them dance—both of them beautiful, unmarried young women—he decided that it was a nice problem to have.

After a while, King Saul stood up, and the musicians ceased their playing, and everyone hushed.

"It's my pleasure to have you all here in my new palace," King Saul said. "Isn't it a lot better to meet on a happy occasion like this than on a battlefield?" The comment got a murmur of agreement from the men in the room, most of whom had led out in the fighting.

"We're celebrating a great victory over the Philistines. We're also celebrating the marriage of my oldest son, Jonathan, to Rahab, an act that will bond the tribes of the north more closely to the kingdom of Israel for years to come."

At that, a cheer went through the crowd. Saul held out his hands for silence.

"Jonathan, as crown prince, has already demonstrated his valor in battle. Now as the future king of Israel, he has the opportunity to show his wisdom. Today I'm appointing Jonathan as executor for the kingdom. When I'm away, he'll be in charge of the daily business that comes with being king."

As applause filtered through the room, Ziba looked at Jonathan's expression, which was like stone. *He'd prefer to be in the thick of it rather than sitting here in the palace deciding where to store grain*, he thought. Saul's intention to keep Jonathan out of battle and out of his hair had resulted in what many saw as an honor. But Ziba knew better.

The music started again, and the female dancers took the floor. Ziba had settled down to watch Michal and Mara when a servant tapped him on the shoulder.

"Pardon me," the young boy said. "But your presence is requested in the meeting hall."

Ziba looked at the table in the front of the room and realized that Saul and Samuel had slipped away. He looked at Jonathan, who remained sitting at the table, a dejected look on his face. Jonathan locked eyes with him and then tilted his head toward the door. Ziba turned and saw that General Abner stood there, gesturing for him to leave with him. Ziba stood up, and the two of them strode out of the feast.

The music behind them, Ziba looked at Abner with a question on his face, but Abner said nothing. They walked quickly down the hall into another large room. King Saul sat there with Samuel and half a dozen of the leaders from other tribes.

"Ah, Ziba," said King Saul. "Come, join us. You're probably wondering why you were asked to be here since your responsibility up to this point has been merely to protect my son in combat."

Merely? Ziba wondered to himself, but said nothing.

"I want you to be here to report to him what we decide," Saul said. "He'll need to know what goes on but will be occupied"—the other men chuckled at that—"for the foreseeable future as a newly married man. You'll be his eyes and ears."

But not mouth, Ziba thought, nodding to the king. *He doesn't want Jonathan's voice heard here.*

"I'll serve as you command," said Ziba, sitting down at a nearby chair.

"Very well," said Saul. "Then on to our first order of business." Saul nodded toward Abner, who had seated himself across from Ziba.

"We have good news and bad news," said Abner. "First the good news. We've amassed a tremendous army. By the last count, we have twenty cohorts of a thousand men each."

"Great news!" Saul nearly shouted. "Right there is the future and protection of our kingdom."

"Our future and protection lie in Jehovah, maker of heaven and earth," corrected Samuel, his forehead creased with disapproval.

"But of course, my apologies," Saul said. "But lands, that's a kingly number."

"And that's the bad news," Abner went on. "Logistics. We need to feed all these men. We need wagons, horses, armor, spears, and swords. We need gold to pay those who stay on.

"In short, gathering such a massive army has bankrupted our kingdom," said Abner. "We're broke."

Saul stood up and walked over to a window that overlooked the garden and the partially finished wall beyond it.

"And I assume that a lavish wedding and building our new capital hasn't helped matters," Saul said quietly. "What are our options?"

"You could announce a heavy tax on the kingdom," said Abner. At that, the tribal elders began to grumble loudly. Saul heard them and turned slightly, nodding.

"We've just gotten them over to our side," he said. "A tax would turn many of them away. What's the other option?"

"Use the men you have," Abner said. "We have armor and weapons for about half the army. Take them and attack Amalek."

"Amalek? Why not Philistia?"

"The Philistine cities are heavily walled and fortified," Abner said. "We don't have the siege equipment to attack them. But Amalek would be much easier to destroy. No walled cities, at least nothing of consequence. If we were to defeat them, we could take lots of plunder and use it to build up our army. In addition, we could hold their generals and king ransom and gain even more gold. Finally, we'd be taking care of a continuous threat on our southern border."

Still standing at the window, Saul turned to see the reaction of the tribal leaders. They all sat, quietly nodding at the idea. He thought about it for a long moment before turning to Samuel.

"Samuel, what do you think? What does God say about such an enterprise?"

The wise old prophet shifted in his seat, first looking at his hands, then looking up at the king through blue, red-rimmed eyes.

"God talked to me last night," Samuel said. "He told me this very thing. Yes, He wants you to attack Amalek and King Agag. But not for the reasons that your general has outlined here.

"God wants to punish them for the difficulties that they gave our people when we came here with our fathers' fathers. They terrorized the children of Israel when they arrived in the Promised Land. They refused to recognize that Jehovah was God of all. And they've remained a thorn in our side since then.

"And so this is what God says. Go up against the Amalekites. Take your army and attack them, and you'll win. Go into battle, and you'll destroy them.

"But God calls for you to destroy them completely. Don't save any sheep, goats, or camels for plunder. Don't leave one man, woman, or child alive. Destroy everything and everyone. They have rejected God and have terrorized God's people. They will all die by flame and the sword. This is the will of the Lord."

The room was silent at Samuel's words; then Abner spoke up.

"But we need the money to save our kingdom," he pleaded.

"You need God more than you need money," Samuel said. "This isn't a request. It's what God requires of you."

Ziba watched as the men around the table stared at Samuel, then at Abner, then at King Saul. Finally, Saul nodded silently.

But even as the meeting broke up and the men went their separate ways, Ziba was unconvinced that the issue had yet been resolved.

Chapter 9

Annihilation

Much like the Philistines, the Amalekites were not farmers or shepherds but merchants and warriors. They would much rather swindle travelers and other merchants than build and sell their own things, and they would rather raid and steal than earn gold and silver themselves.

Amalek was responsible for much more than harassing the children of Israel when they entered Canaan all those years before. They constantly raided every nation around them. They were a thorn in the side of the developing kingdom of Israel as well as every other neighboring kingdom. Saul and everyone else knew that no one would miss them when they were gone.

Attacking the Amalekites was relatively easy. They had never been afraid of Israel before this. On the other hand, Israel had never been able to raise an army of ten thousand armored men before, along with another ten thousand in reserve. Word of the great victory at Michmash had made its way to the neighboring countries, but even with that victory, it was still a great challenge to raise a standing army from a nation of sheepherders.

Knowing this, Saul told Abner to muster the men at Telaim, another small crossroads in eastern Israel. When the men were there, he sent word to the Kenites, a small group of people who had befriended them before they had taken Canaan. He told them that an attack against Amalek was imminent and encouraged them to leave the area.

See 1 Samuel 15 and 16

When they were clear, Saul sent a thousand men with Abner to attack the main encampment. A thousand men was still an imposing force, about the number of men they'd had with them when they attacked Achish at Michmash. It was about the number that Agag would expect to attack his forces, but it wasn't too many for the Amalekites to handle.

The attack was halfhearted, as it was designed to be. After about half an hour of battle, Abner called for a retreat. The entire army of Amalek followed in pursuit, believing that they were about to destroy the Israelite army. Instead, Abner and his men led the Amalekites into a ravine outside the city. There, the remaining nineteen thousand Israelites waited for them.

It was a massacre. Agag lost half his men in the first hour. When he realized what was happening, he called for a retreat. But instead of falling back to his capital city, he fled with his men southward. Egypt had been a strong ally in the past, and Agag hoped they would rescue him and what remained of his army.

They never made it to Egypt. The battle turned into a running slaughter. When it became obvious that the Amalekites had lost their desire to fight, Saul divided his troops. He continued south to finish off the Amalekite army, which he did in grand fashion. At the same time, he sent Abner north to destroy the rest of Amalek in the capital city. He reminded Abner of Samuel's words—that no man, woman, or child should remain alive.

When Saul returned to Amalek to rejoin Abner, the soldiers of Israel were overjoyed. Saul rode into Amalek on his black horse, a beaten and bruised Agag marching on foot behind him, his hands tied and a rope around his neck.

"Who's that you have with you, Mighty King?" Abner said, grinning from the front steps of the palace of King Agag.

"It's a man who claims to be the king of the former nation of Amalek," Saul answered, also grinning. "But he's no longer a king."

"Well said, King Saul," Abner replied.

"How goes the destruction of Amalek?" Saul asked.

"Proceeding as planned," Abner said. "Although it's a shame to put all these horses, fat cows, and sheep to the sword. Especially when we need the money."

"Your general is wise," Agag said, and Saul responded by pulling against the rope around his neck.

"What are you talking about, *former* king?"

"It's a sin against any god, including *your* God, to waste such goodliness," he said. "A lot of good can come from selling these cattle, sheep, and horses. Surely you don't intend to destroy the gold we hold here."

Abner cringed, and Saul frowned. "It's what Samuel commands."

"I thought Saul, and not Samuel, was king of Israel," Agag said. "What will happen to me?"

"Samuel has told us that all men, women, and children of Amalek— including the king—are to be killed."

Agag turned white. "But that's not the way it works with royalty. I have friends in Egypt who will give you ten thousand talents of gold for my ransom. Surely that'll go a long way toward paying for this mighty army of yours."

Saul looked at Abner. "The man has a point," Abner said. "You know we need the money, and you are the king, not Samuel. God wants you to obey, but He also wants you to use your brains."

Saul looked at King Agag, then at the cattle and sheep around him, trying to decide. Finally he nodded.

"All right, Abner," he said. "Keep only the very best livestock. Keep Agag in shackles. When you're done, take a thousand men to Gilgal and meet me there. Dismiss the rest."

"Where will you be?"

A slow grin crept across Saul's face.

"This great victory deserves a monument in our honor."

"In *your* honor, Mighty King," Abner corrected him.

"In *my* honor. I'm going to Mount Carmel to make sure everyone remembers what happened here." And with that, he wheeled his horse and was gone.

Jonathan was never one to sit in silence and wait while major events were unfolding elsewhere. He was commanded to stay in Gibeah and manage the kingdom's daily affairs. But Saul had graciously given him a way to learn what was going on.

Ziba's title remained armor-bearer to the crown prince, but his responsibilities now also included riding back and forth between Saul's army and the capital. When the two of them heard of the victory at Amalek, they expected the army to return right away, especially in light of Samuel's directive. When they heard that Abner was going to Gilgal instead, Jonathan told Ziba that he needed to be there too.

It was several hours' ride to Gilgal, and Ziba made it late in the afternoon. He arrived there just about the same time as an old man on a donkey: Samuel.

Ziba had expected to find a bivouacked army, perhaps preparing for another battle. Instead, he found what looked like a livestock auction. Sheep bleated, and cows bellowed in their pens. On the other side of camp, Ziba heard horses whinnying as well.

Where did all these animals come from? Ziba said under his breath as he dismounted from his horse, and he immediately knew the answer with a sense of dread. Samuel was here to meet with Saul, presumably to congratulate him on his victory. Ziba thought back to that day when they had sat in the meeting room and Samuel had shared his directive. *What would happen now?*

"Samuel!" Saul shouted, throwing his hands in the air, smiling and approaching the old man. "It's good to see you."

"What's this I hear?" Samuel said. "Sheep bleating? Horses whinnying? What's all this?"

Saul paused, then Ziba heard the slightest of stutters. "It's . . . it's a sacrifice to Jehovah for granting us such a great victory."

"And was that a monument to Jehovah that you built on Mount Carmel?" Samuel asked. "Or was it a monument to yourself? Where's the honor here? Where's the glory?"

"Look, we destroyed the rest of the kingdom, just as you asked. We've done what God commanded. Of all the people who lived in the land of Amalek, only King Agag survives."

Samuel's eyes grew large, and Ziba expected him to explode. But Samuel's voice came out quiet and restrained.

"Bring him to me," Samuel said.

As Abner went to get King Agag, Samuel continued to speak.

"Let me tell you what the Lord told me last night," he said, speaking directly to Saul.

"Remember that day when you hid among the baggage, even though the lottery called for you to become king? Remember me anointing you with oil? Even though you were small in your own eyes, look where God has taken you. He sent you on a mission, to destroy the Amalekites. You were supposed to wage war against them until they were completely wiped out."

"But I did do what God commanded," Saul said, a whiny note in his voice. "I did completely wipe out the Amalekites. I only saved King Agag and enough cattle and sheep to have a great sacrifice for God."

"God would much rather have you obey Him than sacrifice to Him," Samuel said. "Doing what you see fit rather than obeying God is arrogance. It's rebellion against God. He told you what He wanted. He gave you a direct command. And now because you've rejected Him, He'll reject you."

The camp was silent except for the lowing of cattle and the bleating of sheep. Finally, Saul spoke again. "What . . . what do you mean?"

Samuel didn't answer but looked at the king with pity on his face. As Ziba watched, the mighty, proud king crumbled before the old prophet.

"Oh, Samuel, I've sinned," he said, falling to his knees. "I admit, I've followed my desires rather than obeying God. I was afraid for the kingdom. I was afraid of my men. Please forgive me, and come back with me."

"No," Samuel said bluntly. "God has rejected you as king. Someone else will take your place." Samuel turned to go.

"No, wait, please," Saul said, reaching out and grabbing the hem of the mantle that Samuel wore. As Samuel pulled away, the fabric tore. Samuel stopped and looked at the king.

"You tore my cloak, but God has torn your kingdom from you," Samuel said. "God has given it to one of your neighbors, someone better than you."

Ziba could see anger mixed with sadness on the prophet's face. Samuel looked around him and noticed Agag kneeling in front of them, next to Abner, just a short distance away. The king had lost his kingdom but so far had saved his own life, and a slight smile played on his lips.

"You're still alive," Samuel said to him.

"Apparently Saul is a king after all," Agag said, an edge of sarcasm in his voice.

Ziba saw the rage rise in Samuel's face and watched as Samuel turned and grabbed Saul's sword. The entire camp watched in horror as the old man raised the sword above his head, then brought it down across the neck of the Amalekite king. As the king's head fell to the ground, Ziba saw a look of total surprise on the face of Agag, king of the mighty Amalekites.

Still in shock, Saul and the rest of his camp stared at the body of King Agag as Samuel got back on his donkey and headed south to Ramah.

"God has given it to one of your neighbors, someone better than you." Ziba thought about those words all the way back to Gibeah. *What did it mean? Where was Jonathan in this new plan?*

He debated on how to share the news from Gilgal, but his long-time friendship called for him to be totally honest with Jonathan. Even though it was late in the evening by the time he arrived, he met with Jonathan, telling him everything.

"The words are puzzling," Jonathan said. "What 'neighbor' is he talking about?"

"The thing that concerns me is that there was no mention of you. Could Samuel have meant you?" said Ziba.

Jonathan paused, then shook his head slowly.

"No. He said that the kingdom was taken from our family. That seems pretty obvious to me that it includes me."

Ziba hardened his mouth and suddenly punched the wall. Dust filtered down from the ceiling.

"It's not fair," Ziba said, and Jonathan could see that he was very close to tears. "You're the bravest, most honorable, most devout man I know. How is it that God can't use you as king?"

Jonathan stared at the corner, shaking his head slowly.

"God's ways are hard to fathom sometimes," Jonathan said. "I've done nothing to earn being king. My father was chosen by God; I wasn't."

"But I assumed . . . everyone assumed . . ." Ziba spluttered.

Jonathan shrugged. "So did I, but, obviously, it wasn't a foregone conclusion with God. What's important is that we serve Him wherever He sends us. I love my God, and I'll serve Him whether I'm the king or a shepherd."

Ziba sighed. "If you're no longer the crown prince . . . or king . . . I won't be armor-bearer. That is, unless a shepherd needs a bodyguard."

Jonathan stood and slapped him on the shoulder.

"You are, first and foremost, my friend. What was that old rhyme you used to share?"

Ziba looked at Jonathan with a lopsided grin.

"Through thick or thin, count me in," he said.

"Whatever you do, I'm with you," Jonathan replied, smiling.

But Ziba couldn't get rid of the feeling that what was happening to Jonathan was unfair. He also selfishly thought that it would remove him from a spot that he'd hoped would make him worthy of Michal. He'd surrounded himself with a royal life, even if he wasn't royalty himself. And now that life was about to leave him.

Or was it? Jonathan didn't seem concerned about the news, but news traveled fast in the palace. Ziba had just risen the next morning and was still fastening his belt while leaving his room when both Mara and Michal met him in the hallway.

"Is it true?" Michal asked. "Is my father being dethroned?"

Ziba took a breath through his nose and hesitated.

"Maybe," he said. "Samuel said that the kingdom would be taken from him, but he didn't say when it would happen. It could be many years from now."

"Or it could be tomorrow," added Michal, looking into the distance.

"Do we know anything about who it is?" Mara asked.

Ziba shook his head. "Samuel only said that it would be given to a neighbor, someone better than your father."

"*Better?*" Michal echoed. "Who could be a better king than my father?"

Ziba didn't answer but looked at Mara, who was thinking the same thing that Ziba was. Saul had had many opportunities to follow God, and Saul had made many mistakes.

"Perhaps it's someone that Samuel has already chosen," said Mara.

"Ziba," Michal said breathlessly. "You need to find out who it is."

"How am I supposed to do that? Samuel isn't going to tell me anything. Besides, I'm here to serve as a messenger for Jonathan."

"*I command you!*" Michal said.

Ziba and Mara looked at each other and burst into laughter.

"Nice try, Michal," Ziba said.

"But I'm the princess!" At that Ziba and Mara laughed even harder. Michal got red in the face, and Ziba could tell she was angry. He realized that he wasn't earning any favor with her by humiliating her. He softened his tone.

"Listen, Michal," Ziba said. "Things are pretty quiet with Jonathan right now. Let me ride down to Ramah and talk to people. See what I can find out. But just know that I'm not doing it because you commanded me. I answer to Jonathan or your father. I'm doing it because . . ." He hesitated to add the final words.

"Because why?" Michal said, leaning toward Ziba.

"Just because."

Ziba had planned on being gone for two days at most, but he was gone for a week. When he returned, Saul had already arrived with Abner and a core of the army that had followed him against the Amalekites. The bulk of the army had been sent home, most of them unpaid.

Mara saw Ziba riding into the stable and promptly ran to get Michal. Before Ziba could climb the steps into the palace, they were upon him.

"What did you learn?" Michal blurted at him. Ziba held up his hand.

"Not here," he said, looking around. "Too many ears. Let's find Jonathan and then I'll tell you."

Jonathan had just finished a meeting with his father in the same hall where they had planned the attack on Amalek. Saul didn't even look at the three young people as they entered the room. Ziba saw that Saul's eyes looked tired and the expression on his face was grim.

Jonathan, however, looked more relieved than anything.

"What have you three been up to?" Jonathan quietly asked. "Ziba, I haven't seen you for a while. Where have you been?"

"I've just returned from Bethlehem," he replied.

"Bethlehem? What's in Bethlehem?" Jonathan asked.

"I sent you to Ramah, not Bethlehem," Michal said, an edge in her voice.

Jonathan looked at his sister, his eyes opening wide, and a slight smile crossed his face as he looked at Ziba.

"You wanted me to find out who the new king would be," Ziba said. "I did . . . sort of."

"What do you mean?" Mara asked.

"I went to Ramah to find Samuel," Ziba explained. "When I got there, he'd already left for Bethlehem. The gatekeeper told me. Interesting what you can learn from gatekeepers, you know."

"Go on," Michal said, impatiently.

"If you've ever been to Bethlehem, you know that there's not much there other than pastures for sheep. I asked around, and a shepherd told me that Samuel had passed through a day before. He'd gone to the house of Jesse. There he'd anointed one of his sons."

Jonathan, Michal, and Mara looked at one another.

"A neighbor," Michal said.

"But get this: the son he anointed?" Ziba continued. "He's just a kid. About twelve. He goes by the name of David."

"So whatever Samuel has planned is bound to happen years from now," Mara said.

"Unless he plans on us having a child for our king," Ziba added.

"It's in God's hands," Jonathan said. "Leave it alone."

"Kid or no, we need to keep an eye on this David," Michal said.

Ziba said nothing but thought it wasn't such a bad idea.

Chapter 10

The Boy Who Would Be King

Ziba didn't see much of Saul after the king's war against the Amalekites and the subsequent fiasco dealing with Samuel. Samuel had been a regular visitor to the capital in Gibeah up to this point, but with the falling out between him and Saul, Samuel became invisible. And Saul took that as a sign that not only was God displeased but God had cursed his reign and all of Israel.

For several years following, Saul began a steady descent into a serious depression. He traveled to his throne room every day but was basically incoherent. Generals, merchants, and officials from the other tribes would come to see him, asking him to intervene on their behalf, but Saul rarely responded. As Ziba watched him, he wondered, then felt convinced that his depression was directly tied to the promise that inevitably he would be replaced as king.

Abner had the best success in rousing Saul from his lethargy. Abner persuaded Saul to begin a campaign to solidify Israel's position throughout the entire region. When they went out to battle, Abner took the lead, with Saul acting as a figurehead, someone whom the Israelites continued to rally around, whether he said anything inspiring or not. And despite Saul's passive approach toward the campaign, the nation of Israel grew more stable.

The best thing that Saul had done turned out to be appointing Jonathan as the king's executor. In addition to his courage on the battlefield, Jonathan turned out to be an excellent administrator. He

See 1 Samuel 16

balanced the nation's budget, finding the funds needed to keep the army going, albeit at a reduced size from the one that attacked Amalek. He negotiated with builders and merchants for the completion of the capital. And more and more, Ziba saw that people were coming to Jonathan instead of the king when they wanted to get things done.

Jonathan also noticed the king's despondency, although he didn't talk to Ziba about it. As a matter of fact, with his new marriage and his new job, Jonathan didn't seem to have much time to talk to Ziba at all.

One day, Ziba was passing the counting room where Jonathan was meeting that day. As usual, Ziba glanced in the open door to see how Jonathan was faring. Jonathan saw him and gestured for Ziba to come in. Surprised, Ziba obeyed and joined Jonathan, who was meeting with Michal and a man he didn't recognize.

"Michal and I've been talking about my father's health. We have been worried about it for some time," Jonathan said to Ziba. "We wondered if music might help him out. I asked Benjamin here," he gestured at the unknown man, "to go looking for a musician who might play for the king. He's just come back."

Benjamin nodded. "I've traveled from Dan to Beersheba," he said. "For a while, I wondered if there was anyone in all of Israel who could play for our king and make him happy. Then I found him."

"That's good," Michal said. "Who is he?"

"A young shepherd boy in Bethlehem," he said. "He plays the lyre and sings like an angel. He also writes his own music."

"Unusual for a shepherd to have the skill necessary to both play an instrument and write music," Jonathan said. "What's his name?"

An instant before the next words came out of Benjamin's mouth, Ziba had a premonition. He glanced at Michal, who seemed to be thinking the same thing.

"His name is David, son of Jesse."

Jonathan looked at Michal, then at Ziba. They silently considered whether this was good news or bad. Then Jonathan nodded his head, making the needed decision.

"Very well," Jonathan said. "Send for the boy."

Benjamin nodded and left. Ziba and Michal waited until the man had left the room. Then Jonathan spoke.

"If he's the one who will someday be king, best to have him here and see what kind of king he'll be."

Or what we can do to prevent it, Ziba added silently.

A few days later Benjamin returned to the palace, a boy of about twelve with him. Ziba was passing by in the hallway, but when he saw that they were heading toward the counting room where Jonathan was holding court, he walked with them.

The boy was slight, not too tall, with curly brown hair and big, grey eyes. He carried a lyre under his arm. He was still dressed like a shepherd, and Ziba could see that the boy had been in the sun quite a bit. Even so, his cheeks were sunburned, making his face look as if he were constantly embarrassed. But Ziba saw something in the child's eyes, both an intelligence that was unusual for a shepherd and a quiet confidence that he'd only seen in one other man before this—Jonathan.

"I understand that you can sing," Jonathan said to the boy when they came into the room.

"I can," David said. "Good enough for my sheep."

Jonathan laughed and Ziba smiled.

"Well, let's see if it's good enough for a king," Jonathan said. "Sing me something."

The boy lifted up his lyre, tuned it for a moment, then strummed it and began to sing: "I will sing of mercy and judgment: unto thee, O LORD, will I sing. I will behave myself wisely in a perfect way. O when wilt thou come unto me? I will walk within my house with a perfect heart . . ."*

David's voice came out sweet and clear, the high voice of a boy who hadn't yet reached manhood. There was something about the boy's voice that made one both restful and long for better days and better things. Ziba and Jonathan looked at each other, and Jonathan nodded.

"You'll do," he said to David. "Come with me." He led David out the doorway and down the hall toward the throne room. Ziba and Benjamin followed at a discreet distance. When Ziba entered the throne room, he saw Jonathan in front of Saul, seated on his throne.

---

* See Psalm 101:1, 2, KJV.

Jonathan's voice was low enough that Ziba could not hear him, but he had a pretty good idea what they were talking about. Finally, Saul nodded, a scowl on his face.

"I don't think it will help, but it won't hurt," he said. "Let the boy sit over in the alcove and play. I don't care."

Both Jonathan and David bowed before Saul and stepped back from the throne. Jonathan led David to a small room off to the side that was open to the throne room, although partitioned by a thin curtain. As Ziba watched them, he could barely see David sitting on a stool there. Jonathan joined Ziba at the doorway, and David began to play. The lyre poured out sweet tones that filled the room, and they both watched Saul for some kind of reaction. After a couple of minutes, they could tell the king was beginning to relax.

Jonathan raised an eyebrow at Ziba, then motioned for him to follow him out the door.

The boy David spent the next few months in the palace, playing for the king every time he fell into a depression. The singing almost always helped Saul rise from the black spell that overwhelmed him. When the depression lifted, Saul was able to function as a king and make decisions that Jonathan was glad to hand over to his father.

When David was not occupied with singing for Saul, he was allowed to roam freely throughout the palace. Ziba was still occupied as an official messenger for Jonathan and occasionally for the king, which meant that he spent a great deal of time on his horse. But there were quiet times for him as well. One of those days, he saw the now thirteen-year-old David standing in the hallway, looking out a window into the courtyard below. Ziba walked up behind the boy and saw what he was looking at.

Mara and Michal sat beside a fountain, talking, not far from where Jonathan had been married some months before. Ziba felt his feelings for Mara beginning to grow, but his longtime decision to marry Michal conflicted within him.

"She's beautiful," David said. Ziba looked at the boy and envisioned him as a future king, someone who was used to fighting for—and getting—whatever he wanted. At first, Ziba wasn't sure which one David was talking about, but then he realized he was talking about Michal.

"Aren't you a little young to be thinking about women?" Ziba asked, raising an eyebrow.

David shook his head. "I mostly spend my time among sheep and singing praises to God. Once in a while, a wolf or a bear creeps into camp, which makes for a bit of excitement. But that never makes me feel the way I feel right now."

Ziba stared at the boy, then shook his head.

"You know, you and I are in the same situation," Ziba said. "We both want something we can't have. Neither one of us is royalty, or even wealthy, for that matter. And so our chances of marrying a princess are between zero and less than zero."

Ziba saw a look of determination come into David's eyes.

"Maybe I won't be a shepherd forever," David said. "If she's not married, maybe I'll have an opportunity to marry her."

"Maybe," Ziba said. "Maybe not." But Ziba could see that David had made up his thirteen-year-old mind.

A week later, Ziba looked out that same window. Michal was sitting at the same fountain, but instead of Mara sitting with her, David was there. Ziba was torn between being amused with the audacity of a thirteen-year-old shepherd boy talking to—perhaps romancing—a princess and a sense of rage that David would set himself up as a rival.

Ziba charged down the stairs, full of anger, but slowed as he neared the bottom. Interfering would go badly with Michal, who never considered the feelings of anyone but herself. She would laugh scornfully at Ziba and then chastise him for feeling threatened by a thirteen-year-old boy. And she was right. There was nothing to be afraid of. A mere boy couldn't seduce Michal.

Ziba stopped at the entrance to the palace and listened to their conversation.

"I'm honored and flattered that you would say those things," Michal was saying. Ziba could see a smile on her lips and could sense that she was trying hard not to laugh at the boy. "But I'm a princess, and you're a shepherd. I'm of marrying age, and you're a boy."

That's right, Ziba echoed in his head. *Just a boy.* He felt relieved that Michal was sharing common sense with David.

"But I'll get older, and soon I'll be a man," David argued. "And I know that I'll feel the same way about you then as I do now. And I won't be a shepherd boy forever."

Michal paused, then forced a smile across her face.

"I suppose when that happens, I might consider your offer."

Chapter 11

The Valley of Elah

Instead of meeting at the stately palace behind the walls of Gath, Zephan planned to meet King Achish on a hilltop a few miles from the city near the town of Socoh. It was a no-man's-land of sorts. Philistines and Israelites kept the other at bay, rattling their swords whenever the other ventured forth into the hot southern desert. Even though the Valley of Elah stretched from Gath for several miles to the east, the city was mostly concerned with trade with the coastal cities to the west. They rarely ventured this way, and that was fine with both parties.

Today, Achish was accompanied by just four bodyguards, who sat on horses at the bottom of the hill. He watched as two horses rode up to meet him from the north. On one was Zephan; on the other was her son, Abner.

"Strange," Achish said. "A Philistine king meeting secretly with the general of all of Israel's armies. Don't you feel a little odd?"

"All I know is that my throat will be cut if they discover we're meeting," Abner said, shifting on his horse impatiently. "Can we get on with it?"

Zephan held out her hand to quiet her son. "I was the one who set up this meeting. It's been thirteen long years since the Philistines and Israel met at Michmash. Thirteen years for Philistia to build its armies again. Isn't that so, Mighty King?" She looked at Achish.

"That's very true," Achish said. "But I learned my lesson the last

See 1 Samuel 17

time. I decided that I needed a secret weapon. And I've found it."

Abner lifted one eyebrow. "Are you sure you want to be telling me this? After all, I'm Saul's right-hand man."

Achish smiled. "I also understand you'd like to be king of Israel. I can make that possible."

"How?" Abner asked, looking at the woman on the horse next to him. "Through my mother's magic?"

"Her magic has grown powerful, that's for sure," Achish said. "But I deal with things I can hold in my hand. Israel has a powerful God, but I've got power as well."

"What kind of power can challenge Jehovah?" Abner asked.

"You leave that to me. Your job is to bring King Saul and his army to this hilltop in the Valley of Elah in one week. When our armies meet, I have a very big surprise for Saul." He laughed at his own words.

"And when you win, I'll be made the king of Israel?" Abner said.

Achish nodded. *As much as that'll be worth*, Achish thought.

It didn't take long for all of Israel to learn that the Philistines were mustering their armies once again. Saul sent out a message for every able-bodied man to join him on the field of battle. But when Philistia threatened Israel at Michmash, that battle was in the middle of the nation. It was harder to get members of Israel's militia motivated to march into the hot desert to confront a mighty army.

Saul pondered this problem as Abner continued to train and equip the soldiers who did arrive. He was running out of time. Abner had told him that Philistia would be marching north in a week. That was five days ago.

"Father," Saul heard as Jonathan entered the throne room. "I still have influence over the northern tribes, both because of my marriage and because of Michmash. Let me come with you to Elah. Maybe more soldiers will come from the north to join us."

Saul shook his head. "You will continue the family line. Your place is here."

"What's the use of a line if the Philistines conquer Israel?" Jonathan asked. "Besides, I have two children, a boy and a girl. You have your heir to the throne."

Saul stared at Jonathan, then nodded. "You're right. Your presence will likely convince more Israelites to join us in battle. You can go." He paused and held up his hand. "But you won't be allowed to fight. You will stay at my side during the entire confrontation."

Jonathan's mouth cut a thin line across his face. "Agreed," he finally said.

Going into battle and standing in the rear wasn't what I had in mind, Jonathan thought. *But who knows what might happen in the heat of battle?*

Ziba felt excited yet nervous, afraid yet elated, when he heard that he and Jonathan were going into battle again. When they attacked at Michmash, it was with an army that was poorly trained and ill-equipped. Not more than one man in twenty had had any weapon worth fearing.

Battle had changed that. And since the embargo on ironsmiths had been lifted, swords, shields, spears, and armor were being mass produced. Every man in Saul's army was armed and armored. Some of that armor had been forged by Ziba's father, Achim.

Ziba rode on his chestnut mare next to Jonathan on his white stallion. He knew that the armor Jonathan wore, shining in the sun, was merely ceremonial. Jonathan had broken the news to Ziba that in exchange for being allowed to attend the battle, Jonathan would be held back. However, both of them were thinking the same thing: *unexpected things happen in battles.*

Most of the soldiers traveling south were veterans from the war against the Amalekites eleven years ago. Many fewer had fought the Philistines at Michmash two years before that. The new troops respected those who had fought at Amalek, but everyone respected the veterans against the Philistines. Ziba heard question after question being passed to The Few, as they were calling those from Michmash. Most were about the Philistines. Rumor and children's stories had helped the Philistines grow in the minds of Israelites who hadn't been to battle against them. And even The Few remembered hiding in caves and running before the might of the Philistines. Rather than encouraging the new soldiers, The Few spent their time warning them not to take the Philistines too lightly.

Ziba looked over at King Saul, who rode his black stallion. Leaving the throne room and going into battle had been good for the king. The years hadn't been kind to Saul, and Ziba again noticed the tic in his left eye. Beside him rode Abner, and behind him, acting as the king's ceremonial bodyguard, was Achim. Their relationship went back to the farmlands of Gibeah, long before a kingdom or a kingship was even thought of. Jonathan had remembered Achim's service to Saul and encouraged him to leave the forge behind and join Saul in battle.

The army assembled on a low rise above the Valley of Elah, which wasn't much of a valley, Ziba thought. But an army always looked for the high ground, and the Israelites needed every advantage they could get. Rumor was that in the thirteen years since Michmash, Philistia had rebuilt its army, almost as powerful as it was during the last invasion. And this time they wouldn't be caught off guard.

Ziba was surprised that the Philistines had already occupied the ridge facing them, perhaps a quarter of a mile away. The valley was broader to the east and west, but this seemed to be the closest that the two armies could get to each other without surrendering the high ground. And both armies insisted on holding on to their real estate.

They spent the next few hours getting organized, with Saul's tent being set up a hundred feet behind the front lines. If the Philistines were to break through, it wouldn't serve as any sort of defense, but it kept prying eyes from knowing what Saul and Abner's plans were. When things were set up, Saul called Jonathan into the tent, and Jonathan motioned for Ziba to join them.

"Well, the first question we'll need to ask is whether it's better to attack them or let them attack us," Abner said. "Perhaps we should wait and see what their plan is before we unveil ours."

"Why wait?" Jonathan said. "If God is with us, who can be against us?"

Saul threw a dark look at his son. "You were invited to come along, and you did your best to encourage troops to join us from the north. But that kind of rash talk will get you sent home."

Jonathan looked at the ground and nodded his head. Ziba was surprised that the new Jonathan was less willing to challenge his father, and he wondered what had changed. Maybe it was his service as an administrator that led him to surrender his will to his father. Ziba hoped that the rash, courageous man who had led him up the rock face and singlehandedly led the charge that won the Battle of Michmash was still in there somewhere.

All of a sudden, a noise ran through the ranks. Saul and Abner looked up, and a moment later, a messenger ran in.

"We have a message from King Achish," the messenger said.

"Well, spit it out, boy," Saul responded.

"He says, 'Why do so many men have to die? Why not settle this like the kings we are? Send out your best man, your champion, and I'll send out mine. Whoever wins will conquer all.' "

Saul looked at Abner and then at Jonathan.

"It sounds reasonable," Saul said. "They have years of battle experience, but we've won a few battles ourselves. Tell him yes."

"Uthai?" Abner suggested.

"Uthai's too old and slow," Jonathan said. "Send me."

Saul shot another dark look at his son. "Don't even think about it."

"How about me?" Ziba said, then immediately regretted it.

Jonathan shook his head. "Serving as my messenger has made you lose your edge. Going up against their best? You're better off staying with me."

Saul looked at Abner. "We don't have a champion, but at least we can see what we're facing."

It didn't take them long to walk up the rise and see the array of Philistines on the other side of the valley. Both flanks were supported by chariots, and Ziba knew that their archers stood behind the armor of the swordsmen and spearmen in the front. Ziba looked and saw that the Israelites were doing the same thing, but instead of using chariots, the Israelites had to rely on mounted troops.

Then a great shout came from the Philistines. Ziba heard them shouting a name:

"Goliath! Goliath! Goliath!"

At first, Ziba thought that his eyes were playing tricks on him. He shielded his eyes from the sun and looked again. What he saw made him gasp.

"Glory, might, and honor," he breathed. Jonathan stood beside him. His mouth became a thin line, and his face turned white.

"Jonathan," Ziba said, "remind me to thank you for not letting me go out there."

As they watched, an armored soldier pushed his way through the ranks and into the front. Ziba saw the head and shoulders of the man—no, *giant*—looming above the next tallest man.

"He must be one of the sons of Anak," Saul said.

"But they're all dead," Ziba said. "Aren't they?"

"Apparently not," Jonathan said. "Achish must have kept this a secret, even from his own army."

"Considering all the information we've gleaned from those soldiers we captured, that's quite an accomplishment."

They watched as the ranks parted and the giant stepped forward. Ziba saw that each step of this giant they called Goliath equaled three of his own. Goliath was clad in heavy iron armor, reinforced with iron straps, something only the son of a blacksmith would recognize. He walked with an iron-tipped spear as a walking stick, and Ziba estimated that it was at least ten feet long. Even so, the spear just barely cleared the head of Goliath.

"Who's that?" Jonathan said, pointing at another man, a lot smaller than Goliath.

"His shield bearer?" Ziba said more as a question than an answer.

"How could he carry that man's shield?" Jonathan shot back as they both saw the immense round bronze shield lying by the giant.

"No clue," Ziba said. "I suspect I couldn't. And that thing is not a man." He turned back and looked at the oncoming warrior. "It's a tower."

As they watched, the giant roared, and everyone on the Israelite side of the valley shook.

"Where is your champion?" he shouted, beating his chest. "I'm here. Come and fight me!"

No one responded. In fact, the entire army of Israel was silent, afraid that anything they said would be interpreted as a willingness to join in combat.

Goliath laughed. "Just as I thought. My brothers and I have never found anyone who could better us in combat. And you are a bunch of cowards! Cowards who worship a weak God!"

Jonathan opened his mouth to respond, but Saul reached out and held him back. Jonathan and Ziba stepped back.

"This does not look good," Ziba said.

The silence continued for more than a month. It was obvious that King Achish was content with goading Saul into sending someone out to fight Goliath. Every day the giant would come out, shouting and stamping up and down the valley in front of the Israelite ranks, just out of range of their archers. Ziba could see that Jonathan was frustrated, but after the first day, Jonathan no longer tried to challenge his father's wishes. Ziba, on the other hand, was more practical and realized that he would be no match for the armored, walking mountain. If Jonathan went, he'd be willing to follow him—and die if need be. But with Jonathan out of the picture, his motivation disappeared as well.

Saul and Abner met constantly, and occasionally Jonathan was called into the meetings as well. At first, Ziba joined him in the discussion but soon realized that their talk was fruitless. Saul began offering gold and even his daughter's hand in marriage to the one who would go out and challenge Goliath. Ziba almost took him up on it, thinking of Michal. But when he thought about volunteering, he grew weak in the knees. He stayed in the middle of the line of Israelites, watching the giant roar and stamp.

While he was there, he became acquainted with three brothers: Eliab, Abinadab, and Shammah. They were from Bethlehem, which wasn't too far away. Ziba heard them bluster to each other, each saying that if Goliath and the rest of the Philistines were to attack, they would kill ten men for each one of them. But none of them volunteered to act as Saul's champion.

After forty days of standing around and listening to the giant roar,

Ziba saw that there was a fourth person with the brothers, a teenaged boy who looked vaguely familiar. He was small but muscular and tanned, his hair bleached by constant exposure to the sun.

"Who is this?" Ziba asked.

"It's just our kid brother," Eliab said. "He should be home tending sheep."

"Father sent me with food for you and anyone else who needs it," the boy said. "What's going on?"

Ziba told him, and as he told of the giant's challenge, he could see the boy's face grow grim. Finally the boy turned and looked at his brothers.

"Why haven't you challenged him?" the boy asked.

"Have you *seen* him?" Abinadab said. "He's twice as tall as you are. He has armor and a sword and a spear. He would kill you without blinking an eye."

"That doesn't matter," the boy said.

"What's your name?" Ziba asked the boy.

"Don't you recognize me, Ziba? I'm David, son of Jesse."

Bells began ringing in Ziba's head. *Could this be the same boy who sang for the king?* David continued to speak out against the giant, and Ziba could see his brothers becoming annoyed. At the same time, others heard David's challenge of Goliath.

"If you're so sure we can beat him, why don't you go out there and challenge him?" Eliab said.

David pressed his lips together and looked out across the valley and at the giant in armor before them. Then he nodded.

"All right, I will," he said.

He's going to get killed, Ziba thought as he led him to the king's tent. *And us along with him.* But Ziba knew that Saul and Abner had not come up with any other plan. And they were running out of time. The intimidation of Goliath would result in Saul's army abandoning him soon.

"Your Majesty," Ziba said as they entered the tent. "This boy, er, man, has offered to serve as your champion. His name is David, son of Jesse."

Saul's eyes grew wide, and Ziba could see a slight grin on Abner's face behind him. *He wants Saul to fail!* Ziba thought. Ziba also saw surprise and recognition on Jonathan's face.

"You don't look like much of a warrior," Saul said to David.

David stood as straight and tall as he could. He was a lot shorter than the very tall king.

"I was enough of a warrior to kill a lion and a bear when they attacked my father's sheep," said David. "King Saul, you have nothing to worry about. Jehovah is with us."

Saul looked at David, then looked at Jonathan and at Abner, who merely shrugged. Then he turned back to David.

"Very well," Saul said. "But you'll need the armor of a warrior. Use mine."

Ziba watched as Saul took off his armor and placed it on David. It engulfed him. He tried walking around with the armor, but he could hardly move. The teenager looked more like a boy than ever before.

"No," David finally said, pushing the armor off. "I'm not used to that armor. This Philistine is no different than the lion and bear. Let me fight him in my own way."

Saul stared at the boy, and Abner shook his head. Ziba saw that Jonathan was watching David warily, and he could see a sense of admiration for David's courage coming onto Jonathan's face.

"Very well," Saul said, with a note of sadness in his voice. "Perhaps Jehovah is indeed with you. Perhaps He'll give you victory. We've got no other choice."

David walked toward the front lines of the army, and Saul, Abner, Jonathan, and Ziba walked with him. They saw that Goliath and his shield bearer had walked toward the Philistine lines. Ziba found his place next to David's brothers, who muttered among themselves, torn between anger at David's boldness and concern about David's safety. As they watched, David walked down to the bottom of the ravine in front of them.

It had rained the previous day, and a small stream ran the length of the valley. David paused and knelt down.

"What's he doing?" Eliab asked no one in particular.

Ziba saw him pick up something out of the streambed.

"Stones," Ziba said. "He picked up five stones." He looked at

Jonathan, who had joined them. "Why stones? And why five?"

Jonathan looked at Ziba grimly.

"Maybe he knows something we don't know," Jonathan said. "Goliath talked about his brothers. Maybe there are more giants over there."

Ziba turned and faced the Philistine lines. "Yep, he's going to get us all killed," he said.

As they watched, David began walking toward the Philistines. The giant Goliath had his back to David, but his shield bearer got Goliath's attention and pointed out David's approach. Goliath turned and did a double take when he saw who had taken the role of Israel's champion.

"What, you think I'm a dog? Are you going to pelt me with *rocks*? Hah! Come over here and die, you little boy. The vultures and the wolves will eat well tonight."

"They sure will," David shouted back at Goliath, loud enough for Ziba and the rest of the army of Israel to hear. "But it won't be my body they'll eat. You've got your armor, your spear, and your shield. But I have something much more powerful."

Goliath laughed. "And what's that?"

"I've come out here with Jehovah, the God of Israel. I may be small; I may be without armor and sword. But He is going to give me victory. And I'm going to cut off your head this afternoon."

Goliath heard the words, shook his head, and then roared. As Ziba watched, Goliath pulled back his helmet so he could see, then started running full tilt toward David.

"Here it comes," Jonathan said.

David didn't hesitate, but starting running toward Goliath as well. While he ran, he reached into a bag on his waist and recovered a stone. With his other hand, he pulled out a sling. Placing the stone in the small patch of leather in the middle of the sling, David began to swing the sling round and round above his head. Faster and faster it twirled, with David and Goliath quickly running to meet each other.

Then Ziba saw David let go of one end of the sling. Faster than the eye could follow it, the stone flew through the air. As Ziba and the rest of the army of Israel watched, the stone hit the giant Goliath square in the forehead, exactly where he'd been armored just a few moments before. Goliath took another step, then collapsed to the ground.

Both armies were shocked. David ran until he reached Goliath's side, then he pulled out Goliath's tremendous sword. Holding it above his head, David dropped it on Goliath's neck, lopping off Goliath's head in one blow. Blood gushed freely from the body and head. Then David raised the severed head up for the two armies to see. Without any question, Goliath was dead.

The two armies were silent for a long moment. Then Ziba spoke up. "What are we waiting for?" he shouted. "Let's go!"

He ran down the hillside, sword in hand, toward the valley and the Philistine front lines with the rest of the army of Israel following. A moment later, the proud Philistine army began running in the other direction.

It was another rout.

Chapter 12

The Usurper

L oaded down with loot from their victory over the Philistines, the army of Israel returned to Gibeah ready for a celebration.

What they got was more than they anticipated. Word of their victory—David's victory—had spread throughout the kingdom. In a few days, David had become the superstar of the kingdom of Israel. Thousands came from all over Israel not only to congratulate the king and his army for their overwhelming victory but also to get a glimpse of the boy who killed the giant that no one else would confront.

Most of the army took it in stride and welcomed the celebration, even though they heard the name of David shouted many, many times as they marched down the street. But a few were caught off guard and somewhat offended. One of those was Ziba. He was staunchly supportive of Jonathan and the family of Saul, even though deep down he knew that Saul was leading his nation in the wrong direction. But even so, he longed for the day when Jonathan would assume the throne, believing that the new king would correct all that Saul had done wrong.

Ziba looked over at Saul, riding on his black horse, and saw that he was having a problem with the crowd's response to David's victory. His face puckered when the two of them heard the same thing, coming from a line of young, beautiful women lining the street.

"Saul has killed a thousand men, but David has killed ten thousand."

Ziba heard the words chanted over and over, and though he knew it was more a song of victory and celebration, he could see how Saul

See 1 Samuel 18

could take it as a taunt. He watched as the dark cloud engulfed Saul, just as it had done in his throne room over the past years.

When the victors arrived in the palace, the servants hurried to welcome them, ushering the dust-covered men into their apartments for baths and a change of clothes. Ziba didn't have any servants because technically he was one himself. But he arrived at his room just as he saw Mara stepping out of it, a faint wisp of a smile on her lips. Neither one said anything. He passed her and shut the door.

In the center of the room was a large tub filled with water. Ziba unbuckled the straps on his chest plate, letting it fall to the floor; removed his greaves, leggings, and undergarments; and stepped toward the tub. He dropped into the water of the tub, expecting it to be cold, or at least lukewarm. Instead he was welcomed by a hot bath, a luxury only royalty could afford. He sighed as he sank into the water, grateful that Mara had done this wonderful thing for him.

Later, clean and dressed, Ziba stepped out into the hall. He was welcomed by a young boy who bowed before him. Surprised, Ziba bowed back.

"I'm here to tell you that a banquet has been prepared in your honor."

"My honor?" Ziba echoed, smiling.

His words caught the boy off guard, and he stammered. "I mean, in honor of the army that has defeated the Philistines."

Ziba nodded and followed the boy down the hallway. In the banquet hall, he saw places set for the officers who had served in the victorious army, including Achim and Abner. At the front of the room, a table welcomed King Saul, Prince Jonathan, and the new member of the palace, David, who sat next to Jonathan.

David seemed a little embarrassed at all the uproar. In addition, it seemed like every young woman—and some of the older ones—fawned over the new warrior when they came by the table. Jonathan even saw Michal staring at him and blushing.

But now that they were clean and dressed, Ziba saw that the boy had become a young, virile man. He was dressed in Jonathan's clothes, which made sense because the only clothes he had with him were those of a shepherd. But Ziba still bristled at the thought of David wearing the clothes of the crown prince. As he watched, he saw Jonathan lean into David, telling him something in confidence, and the two of them laughing. And Ziba felt jealousy rise in himself.

Ziba scanned the table and saw that Saul was bothered by all the attention as well. The king was used to having all eyes focused on him. But David's celebrity had raised him in the estimation of the nation of Israel, while the victory, one that Saul felt should be his, was given to another.

Then Jonathan stood up. "We're here to celebrate a great victory over our rivals to the west. But I know that, more importantly, you're here to see the one who gave us that victory, who did what no other man could do. I give you David, the giant killer."

He gestured with his open hand to the boy who sat beside him. The crowd of officers and their servants went wild, clapping and cheering. In response, his cheeks red with embarrassment, David held up one hand and nodded.

"David, son of Jesse, is no longer just a subject of our kingdom, or a soldier in our army. He's now a member of the royal family. And as a symbol of that acceptance," Jonathan reached behind him and pulled out his weapons, "I give him my sword and my bow. It's not right that a royal family member rely on a sling as his only weapon."

"He did pretty well with just a sling," an officer shouted from the back. The others laughed, as did Jonathan. Ziba could see a faint smile even on Saul's lips, but then it disappeared quickly.

"He'll be trained as a soldier, armor will be made for him, and he'll be given the proper respect of any other member of our family. Because he doesn't have appropriate clothing yet, he'll wear mine until he has clothes made."

Ziba heard a whisper run through the crowd, and the idea rankled him. He'd assumed that David wearing Jonathan's clothing at the banquet was temporary, but for him to offer his clothing on a regular basis was to put David on equal footing as the crown prince. *This is getting out of hand*, he thought.

After the banquet, while everyone was filing out of the hall and returning to their quarters, Jonathan stopped Ziba in the hall.

"Ziba, I have an important task for you," Jonathan said. "I want you to take charge of David's training in weaponry." Ziba looked behind Jonathan at David, who was still fighting off admiring women and embarrassment. Jonathan turned to David. "Ziba is an old friend, and one of our finest servants."

Servant? Ziba thought. This was the first time in his life he'd heard Jonathan call him that.

Ziba fought down anger and then took a deep breath and bowed.

"Whatever pleases Your Majesty," he said.

Ziba spent the following weeks training David in swordplay and in the use of a bow, a spear, and a javelin. He showed him how a shield could be an offensive weapon as well as defensive. And to his dismay, Ziba saw that David was a quick study. Within weeks, David could spar with and defeat the best warriors that Israel put in front of him.

Word of this spread throughout the palace, and it only helped increase everyone's adulation of David. Ziba watched the way Michal looked at David whenever she passed by, and how her eyes showed an affection that Ziba had never seen before. Ziba's jealousy rolled inside of him, and even though he knew that it was wrong and unfair to Jonathan, he embraced it. *The boy had killed a giant that not even I was willing to face*, he told himself. *But he wasn't the only soldier there.*

David's skill as a soldier grew and grew until Ziba discovered that he really didn't have a lot more to teach David. At that point, Ziba invited him into strategy discussions with Saul's officers. David listened for a couple of weeks, and then one day Ziba discovered that David was taking part in the discussion.

After three months of training David, Ziba was called to meet with King Saul. Ziba expected that the king would either congratulate Ziba on his excellent training or send him on another messaging task.

Instead, he met Saul in an otherwise empty throne room.

"Ziba, you've been training the young boy for the past few months." Ziba noticed that Saul didn't call David by name. "How is he doing?"

"Very well, sir. He's exceeded all expectations."

"Has he?" Saul said. There was a pause as Saul looked off in the distance. "He's been shown favor by my son, Jonathan, favor that I'd neither expected nor approved of. You've been a friend of Jonathan's for many years, ever since you were boys playing in the dirt. Tell me, honestly, what you think of this David."

Ziba paused, realizing that the next words he spoke could be important to his future.

"He is charismatic, brilliant, and courageous," Ziba said. "At the same time, he's presumptuous and has no regard for class or respect for his elders."

Saul hesitated, and then spoke, his voice a little softer than before.

"Do you think he could be a threat to the throne?"

Ziba thought of what they had discovered years before and of how David had captured the admiration and imagination of Israel since his victory.

"Yes, Your Majesty, he might."

Saul's anger showed on his face. "They shout out, 'Saul has killed a thousand men, and David has killed ten thousand.' And someday he might take my throne. How's that supposed to make me feel? Me, the king of Israel? But I can't just kill him." He looked up at Ziba. "What should I do about it?"

Ziba paused again. To conspire against David would be to alienate Jonathan, a lifelong friend. And yet Jonathan had already pushed him aside.

"You can't just send him away," Ziba said. "If you did, it would alienate your son and the whole nation. What I'd suggest, Your Majesty, is to draw him closer. Make him officially a part of your family—or at least offer to. Then as a price for that reward, require him to do something impossible. Something very dangerous."

Saul thought about Ziba's words, staring off into the distance, then nodded.

"Good advice, young friend," King Saul said. "I'll make him not only part of the family but commander of a cohort. I'll send him into battle. Let the Philistines kill him. Then I won't have to." He looked up at Ziba, squinting his eyes as if seeing him for the first time.

"Ziba, I'd like to make you a regular consultant. Keep your eyes and ears open, and report to me whenever there are any developments regarding this David."

Ziba nodded and stepped away from the throne and left the room.

He felt dirty by conspiring against David and Jonathan. And yet, like King Saul, he felt that David was more of a danger than anyone else recognized.

Rumors of Saul's jealousy of David circulated through the palace. Ziba heard it from one of the guards outside the king's throne room. One day, Ziba watched closely as he waited for an audience with Saul to report the status of his army on the northern border. The king sat listening to David's music.

"Blessed is the one
    who does not walk in step with the wicked
or stand in the way that sinners take
    or sit in the company of mockers,
but whose delight is in the law of the LORD."*

Ziba watched the king and could tell that something was wrong. Saul held his spear shaft, head down, and Ziba could see his knuckles grow white as he clenched it. Behind the king and to one side, Ziba could see Abner standing, a faint smile on his lips. *He knew something!*

As Ziba watched and David sang, it was as if a black cloud enveloped King Saul, and Ziba felt as if an evil presence had entered the room. Ziba gasped at the change in Saul's expression. Depression turned to a scowl, then a total rage. He hadn't seen that expression on Saul's face since the battle of Michmash. He looked like he was ready to explode.

And he did. With a roar, Saul leaped to his feet and raised the spear,

* See Psalm 1:1, 2, NIV.

its head pointed in David's direction. Saul threw the spear directly at David.

Ziba had seen the king practice the art of throwing javelins and knew that he was equally adept at throwing spears. He rarely missed the mark, and when he did, it was less than an inch or two off target. At that moment, Ziba realized that David was a dead man—or boy.

But Ziba had not counted on the agility of David. The boy fell to the ground, and the spear sailed by, inches from his head, embedding itself in the plaster behind him.

The throne room fell into an uproar. Saul was immediately surrounded by his soldiers, including Abner, who whisked the king away, afraid for his life. Ziba, on the other hand, knew that David was the one in danger. He ran to the side of the boy, who still lay on the floor, his lyre lying next to him.

"I'm OK, I'm OK," David said. Ziba helped him to his feet, his eyes still watching the king as he was hurried out of the room. Michal and Mara came to David a moment later, and the three of them hurried David out of a different entrance. Ziba led them directly to Jonathan's counting room, where Jonathan was talking to a merchant. When Jonathan saw the looks on their faces, he dismissed everyone from the room.

Breathlessly, Ziba and Michal told Jonathan what had happened. Jonathan sat listening, not reacting until the end. Then he nodded solemnly.

"It's those dark spells Father has," Jonathan said. "I've watched him over the months, and they're getting worse."

"We'd hoped that music would calm him," Michal said.

"And it did, for a while," Jonathan said. "But he's been thinking about his separation with Samuel and his separation from God. As well he should."

"This can't go on," Ziba said.

Jonathan nodded. "Knowing what we know about David's future, it'd be wrong to endanger him by leaving him here. It would be a sin against Jehovah."

Ziba was torn between agreeing with Jonathan and a faint hope that David's death would restore his chances with Michal. But he dismissed that thought as quickly as it appeared.

"What do we do?" Ziba asked instead.

"Here's what we'll do," Jonathan answered. "We get David out of the palace as soon as possible. Ziba, you make sure it happens."

"And what do we tell your father?"

"Let me handle my father," Jonathan said. "This madness has to stop."

Ziba agreed with Jonathan, but he also worried about Jonathan's life.

A few days later, Ziba ran into Mara in the hall. Her face was shining, and Ziba was surprised.

"What's happening?" Ziba asked. "Why are you smiling like that?"

She blushed and then smiled more broadly.

"I just received the news. The crown prince has made me Michal's chief handmaiden."

Ziba smiled at her. "That's good news."

She nodded. "I'm still a servant, but now I know I won't be bouncing around, working in the kitchen one day, sweeping floors the next, and drawing water the third. And I get to spend all my time with my best friend." She then blushed, glanced at Ziba, then looked at the floor.

"Well, one of my best friends."

"That's wonderful news, Mara," Ziba said. "I'm happy for you."

She then paused as if to change the subject.

"Have you heard the other good news? The palace is buzzing."

Ziba shrugged. "The palace is always full of gossip. I don't pay attention to it."

"This isn't gossip. I heard it from the baker, who heard it from a guard, who heard it straight from his commander."

Ziba smiled at that. "Go on."

"David has been given a cohort. It's smaller than most, but he gets to pick his men. They'll be going out on assignment soon."

Ziba shrugged. "David's a smart man. Courageous too."

Mara's eyes shone. "And King Saul has pledged his oldest daughter, Merab, to him in marriage."

Ziba smiled to himself. Merab was at least ten years older than David, and Michal was far prettier. He wondered how Michal felt about the match, and how David felt. All he knew was that he still had hope to one day have Michal.

The news turned out to be short-lived. A few days later, he learned that David had refused the king's offer, saying, "Who am I? I'm nobody, a shepherd. I don't even come from a respectable family. And you want me to marry your daughter?" And so Saul betrothed Merab to Adriel, a merchant from Meholah in the north. Ziba knew the man had done business with Jonathan.

However, David agreed to assume command of a cohort, and Saul sent him into battle after battle. They soon learned that David was a natural commander. He fought many battles, especially against the Philistines. Each time he led his cohort from the front, and each time he returned to the capital victorious. And so his fame grew.

Ziba saw David's continuing time spent in combat as an opportunity to try once again to win Michal over. But when he talked to her, all she could talk about was David. At first, Ziba listened to her patiently, but after a while he found himself avoiding her, simply because he couldn't bear to hear the name of David one more time.

And then David returned from another victory, this time over Nob, one of Achish's top generals. David and his cohort had crushed him in the desert of Negev, leaving just a few soldiers alive to tell the tale of their defeat. Again there was a victory dinner in their honor, but when Ziba looked in on the festivities (to which he hadn't been invited), he saw that David wasn't there.

On a hunch, he went out to the garden where he'd seen David with Michal four years ago. Sure enough, the two of them sat by the fountain, talking. And once again, Ziba crept down the stairs to an alcove nearby and listened in on their conversation, peeking around the corner just enough to see without being seen. It was a storybook setting, with singing birds and the sound of bubbling waters filling the air. David was singing quietly to her.

"My dove in the clefts of the rock,
   in the hiding places on the mountainside,
show me your face,
   let me hear your voice;
for your voice is sweet,
   and your face is lovely."*

Ziba watched as Michal blushed and David smiled in return.

"Do you still think I'm too young?" he heard David say, leaning into her.

"You're younger than I am," she said, smiling faintly.

"And yet I'm old enough to command my own force of soldiers. And from what I understand, captain them well."

"Yes, you do that. You're a great captain," she said, nodding. "It's just that . . ."

"Just that what?"

She hesitated and moved away slightly. "Maybe it's because I'm too old for you."

David scoffed, then he reached out his hand and placed it on hers.

"I once told you that I was in love with you. If that's changed, it's that I'm more in love than ever before."

"But why? You have so many who love you. You could have any woman you desire."

"I desire you," David said, his voice rising. "I always have, and I always will."

Michal paused. "And I desire you, David. I desire you and want to be your wife."

The words cut through Ziba's heart like a knife. He turned away from the garden and crept back up the stairs. Mara was standing at the top and noticed Ziba's face clouded in pain.

"What's wrong with you?" Mara said.

"It's nothing. Now leave me alone."

"Are you in pain? Is there something I can do for you?"

Ziba scowled. "No, there's *nothing* you can do for me. Now leave."

Mara looked behind him and down the stairs.

* See Song of Songs 2:14, NIV.

"You've been listening to the two of them," she said, turning back to him. "You're learning something I've known for some time. That her heart belongs to someone else."

"She's making a mistake."

"Is she?" Mara said. "Or maybe you're the one who's making a mistake. Maybe you've been mistaken for years. She's told you—a lot of people have told you—that she'll never marry you. But you're just discovering the truth today. You don't deserve her. You deserve someone else, someone who loves you for who you are."

"And who would that be?" Ziba said, looking down, his face still dark.

"You're close enough to touch her, and yet you're blind."

Mara waited for Ziba to respond, a flush of embarrassment touching her cheeks. Finally he looked up, his face still clouded.

"You're talking in riddles, and I don't have time for them."

Mara stared at him. "Then you're a fool."

He shouted back at her. "And who do you propose I marry? You? Ha! That'll be the day." He regretted the words as soon as he said them.

Mara's face grew red. "If you want to be left alone, then you'll stay alone. Maybe for the rest of your life." She turned and stomped away.

Ziba stared down the stairs at his rival and the woman he loved. Something had to happen. He couldn't let Michal go to another.

He thought about what he should do, and one word came to his mind.

Saul.

Chapter 13

The Heart of a Fool

David and his cohort continued to chalk up victory after victory. Even though they never lost a battle against any of the nations that they fought, their skirmishes against the hated Philistines were the most significant. And every time they returned to Gibeah, the crowd of people there to welcome them was greater than before.

As David's popularity grew, Ziba grumbled inside himself. He began to wonder if the new commander had some kind of spell over him that made him invincible. *Yes,* he thought, *that would explain why he was so willing to face the giant all those years before.*

One day, Ziba was surprised to be summoned into the counting room to see Jonathan. It had been a long time since the two of them had been together, and he thought that Jonathan perhaps missed those times. He knew he did. Despite being surrounded by others who seemed to care about him, he felt alone. He was thinking about this when he entered the counting room. David stood with another young man across the table from Jonathan.

"Ziba, old friend," Jonathan said. "Come in."

"What can I do for the crown prince?" Ziba mumbled, remembering their last encounter.

"Oh, come on now, Ziba," Jonathan said, standing and walking over to Ziba. He reached out and hugged him. "It's been too long. We need to go into battle together. I know I'm not allowed to do that anymore, but maybe we can at least go hunting again."

See 1 Samuel 18

Ziba brightened. "I'd like that."

Jonathan pulled away. "So would I, my friend. I want you to meet someone." He turned toward David.

"David you know. This is his nephew, Joab. He's from Bethlehem as well. David has made Joab his second in command."

Ziba reached out his hand and shook Joab's. "Welcome," he said simply.

"Now if you're done with us, Jonathan, we'll take your leave," David said.

Jonathan nodded. "Be safe, brother."

David nodded and left, Joab at his side. Jonathan watched them exit and turned back to Ziba.

"That's one remarkable young man," Jonathan said. "No matter how much danger is before him, he still comes out on top."

"To tell you the truth, it's kind of irritating," Ziba said, then caught himself.

Jonathan raised one eyebrow. "What do you mean?"

Ziba bowed. "Forgive me, Prince. I spoke out of turn."

Jonathan slapped Ziba on the shoulder. "That's enough of that, Ziba. You're my first best friend. That'll never change."

Ziba let out a breath and smiled at those words. "That's what I wanted to hear."

"Of course. How could you think any different?" Jonathan said, then turned and looked in the direction that David had gone. "Him? Can't a man have more than one best friend?"

No. I don't think so. "Sure. I guess," Ziba said.

"Now what did you mean that David irritates you?"

"He never gets hurt. He gets what he wants. Always. Everything seems so—"

"Easy? Simple to him?" Jonathan said. "I doubt it's ever that simple. But he has a strong faith in God, something that I envy, something that I hope I'll someday learn to have." Jonathan stared again out the doorway, then turned to Ziba.

"There's something I want you to have, old friend." Jonathan reached into a pocket and pulled out two silver rings. They each had a red stone on the front with an etching of a hawk. He gave one to Ziba.

"I had these made to commemorate Michmash. They're identical.

That's something you and I will always share."

Ziba put his on and looked at it, then shook his head. "Jonathan, you've always been my hero. You're a man of God. Even if it's not God's plan for you to be king, you'll always be leader to me."

Jonathan continued staring out the doorway. "Through thick or thin," he said.

Ziba smiled. "Count me in."

The next day, King Saul summoned Ziba to the throne room. As before, he dismissed everyone else out of the room and then beckoned Ziba to come closer.

"That young man David is unbreakable," Saul said. "And he has no fear. What do you think is his secret?"

Ziba's jealousy rose again, and he said something that he would regret later. "I've heard that he has a spell cast upon him. A witch has made him impervious to spears, arrows, and the sword."

"A witch? Are there witches in my kingdom?"

Ziba nodded. "I've heard of a few."

"What can I do about it?" Saul asked. "I know. I'll order that all witches in the kingdom be killed. I'll tell Abner to make it happen. That'll fulfill God's will as well as my own."

Then he leaned forward again.

"I've heard that my daughter Michal is infatuated with that usurper."

Ziba hesitated, then nodded. "He's told her that he loves her, and she loves him."

Saul sat back on his throne. "What do you propose I do about it?"

Ziba cleared his throat. "*Propose* is probably the right word to use here. Maybe what you need to do is ask David what his intentions are, and then give him a price for her that he needs to pay. A price that's too high for even David."

Saul thought to himself, then nodded. "Well said, Ziba. Thank you."

Ziba left the king's presence thinking, *Have I done the right thing?*

That same day, he heard the news. Saul had agreed to give Michal's hand to David in marriage. But the price was staggering: he had to kill one hundred Philistines and collect their foreskins—something only a non-Israelite could provide—as proof that they'd been killed. Ziba was stunned. David had shown his prowess in battle, leading his cohort to victory after victory, besides killing the giant who had terrorized the entire army. But with Goliath, he'd had the element of surprise and had used it to his advantage. Killing a hundred Philistines would afford him no such luxury. And if he killed them, he still had to collect their foreskins, which would be impossible if there were any more Philistines around.

As David was preparing for the expedition to the south, Ziba was summoned to Saul's chamber.

"Ziba, I've always been able to count on you," Saul said. "I want you to go with David and report to me what you see."

Ziba gulped but nodded. "As you command, Your Majesty."

David was surprised when Ziba appeared. He was preparing for the trip with Joab, who insisted on coming with him. Ziba shrugged and told him the truth.

"King Saul wants me to go with you and report on what I see," he said simply.

David smiled. "Very well. If my father-in-law-to-be wants to see me in action, then that's what he'll see." He hesitated. "Or at least hear about."

Early the next morning, the three of them lay on their chests on a rise overlooking a military compound near Socoh that Ziba knew was filled with Philistines. Apparently, a strange look came over his face because Joab asked him what was wrong.

Ziba smiled faintly. "Nothing. I just remembered doing this with Jonathan, too many years ago."

David smiled. "Then you should be a veteran of this kind of thing. Here's the plan. The king wants me to collect the foreskins, not you two. So I'll take the lead."

"Where do you want us?" Joab asked.

"You two will protect my backside and make sure they don't get behind me."

Joab nodded, but Ziba hesitated.

"You only need one hundred foreskins, but there are well over two hundred soldiers in there."

"Then we'll just have to bring back two hundred foreskins," David said, smiling. "Besides, Michal is worth it."

Indeed she is, Ziba thought.

Ziba had seen a lot of men in combat, and he'd heard stories of how David fought and led others to fight. He never wore armor but preferred the tough leather that the Israelites used to wear. Now Ziba learned why.

David crept closer and closer to the two men stationed by the entrance to the compound. Soon he was within a stone's throw of them.

"That's far enough," Ziba whispered from the rise.

"Maybe for you," Joab said. "David likes to be close enough to spit on them."

Sure enough, David continued creeping forward. Ziba was sure that David would be seen. Instead, David reached into his quiver and pulled out an arrow. He rose, quickly pulling back the bowstring and releasing the arrow. Because there was such a short distance to travel, by the time the second guard noticed the arrow sticking out of his partner's chest, the second arrow was on its way. Both men collapsed to the ground without making a sound.

Then David did the same thing to the two isolated guards within the towers. Again, there was no sound. Finally, he gestured for Ziba and Joab to join him. To Ziba's dismay, David was already inside, immersed in fighting, by the time they arrived at the gates.

Ziba stood in amazement at David's quick, fluid actions. He anticipated every action that the Philistines would make before they made it. Within a minute, a dozen men lay dead at his feet. The others were slow in getting up, most of them still not knowing what was happening, simply because David's death strikes came with very little noise.

But after several minutes, as the dead continued to pile around him, the Philistines realized what was happening, and circled around to attack David from the rear. Once again, Ziba had a sense of déjà vu, remembering the battle above the cliffs of Michmash. That morning, he and Jonathan had changed the fate of Israel. Could this be a similar event? Ziba watched David kill and kill again, and then with a growing sense of pride, took on his role as the rear guard. He knew how to use a shield and spear, even if it had been a while since he'd last fought. But when death was at your door, he knew, it didn't take long to remember.

The battle grew hot, and the Philistines continued to press from behind. But Joab was a worthy partner, and he and Ziba were able to hold them off. Whenever Ziba found a break in the onslaught, he looked over his shoulder to see how David was faring. Inevitably, they would find that David had moved forward, leaving them behind. Then they would have to lower their shields and spears and run over to where he was. They weren't there to kill Philistines; that was David's job. But they were there to protect him, and they had to be where he was to do that.

The morning wore on—or seemed to. When the numbers of the Philistines started to get smaller, Ziba looked around them, and then at the sun. As far as he could tell, what seemed like half a day had happened in less than an hour. The ground around them was piled high with Philistine bodies. Ziba and Joab were exhausted and out of breath. They had cuts and bruises all over their bodies, but David was unscathed. Indeed, he seemed like he'd just finished a vigorous dance, and was ready for more.

"Oh, to have his energy," Joab muttered. Ziba looked over at David's nephew and realized that he wasn't the only one who was amazed at David's prowess.

"What are you two waiting for?" they heard David shout, even though they were only a few feet away. "We have foreskins to collect."

King Saul was amazed when David, Ziba, and Joab returned to his throne room just one day after they had left. David carried a wooden box under his arm. When Saul called them forward, David bowed before him, and the others followed suit.

"What do we have here?" Saul asked, gesturing toward the box. "Are these the hundred foreskins I asked for?"

"No, Your Majesty," David said. "A hundred foreskins was too small a price to pay for your daughter, the woman I love. And so I have brought you two hundred foreskins."

Ziba heard the crowd behind him gasp. David lifted the lid and showed Saul the layers of cut skin that lay inside.

"Feel free to have Abner count the number. But I assure you, there are two hundred there."

Saul furrowed his brow and looked at David. Then he turned to Ziba.

"Is this true? Did he kill two hundred Philistines to gain this prize?"

Ziba nodded. "It's true. I was there, protecting him from behind." Saul started to say something, but Ziba added. "We protected him, but the Philistines were all killed by David."

The audience gasped again, then a small round of applause started. Saul looked around the room, a scowl on his face, and applause stopped. Then he turned to David.

"It seems that you've kept your end of the bargain. Now I have to keep mine. You shall marry my daughter Michal."

Another gasp, and the applause was a lot louder this time. Ziba saw an immense grin come upon David's face. He bowed to Saul.

"Thank you, Your Majesty. I'll make you a great son-in-law and provide you many grandchildren."

"Just take good care of my daughter," Saul said.

"That I will."

It took a month to send out all the announcements regarding David and Michal's wedding as well as make preparations. While Jonathan's wedding had been a big affair—the biggest celebration the fledgling nation had previously seen—it was dwarfed in comparison to Michal's. Israel wasn't a rich kingdom like Egypt or Philistia, but Saul spent every spare penny he could find on food, flowers, and decorations.

And Michal, who had been looking forward to this day her entire life, wouldn't have it any other way.

Because Samuel was unwilling to return to Gibeah as long as Saul was there, the king officiated for the ceremony. The bride was beautiful, though covered in the traditional fine linen. David, now the owner of his own wardrobe, wore a gold tunic and pants with a red sash. Many women and young girls sighed in regret that David would no longer be an eligible bachelor, but most everyone agreed that he and Michal seemed right for each other. Jonathan stood in the front row of onlookers, a smile on his face that seemed like it would never go away.

Ziba found himself at his usual place, in the window overlooking the garden. He expected Mara to appear, as she always seemed to do, but she never did. When they followed the wedding with the usual banquet, he pulled Jonathan aside.

"Aren't they a good-looking couple?" Jonathan said. "It's as if they were fated to be together."

"I thought you didn't believe in fate," Ziba said, not totally in agreement on how great they looked together.

"I might not, but an event like this might challenge that belief."

"Where's Mara?" Ziba blurted out.

"She's not here," Jonathan said. "Why do you ask?"

"I . . . I just am used to seeing her at these kinds of events. And she was close to Michal. I'm surprised she's not here to congratulate her."

"Mara's gone."

"Gone? Gone where?"

"She's gone home. To Jabesh-gilead."

"Why?" Ziba asked, more to himself than to Jonathan.

"Don't you think it's a little late to be asking about Mara? Where were you when she was here?"

"What are you talking about?" Ziba asked, knowing the answer before Jonathan said it.

"She's in love with you, Ziba," Jonathan said. "I always thought you were blind when it came to love. You spent years pining after that sister of mine, and here you go and pass up a good thing like Mara. Where's your head, man?"

That's a good question, Ziba thought to himself.

Chapter 14

A Conflict of Interest

D avid had just returned from another victory in the south against the Philistines. He was walking back to his apartment to wash the dust off himself when Ziba saw him. The boy had become a man; no, a leader. He carried himself with a confidence that made those around him feel more assured. He listened to advice from several sources before making his decisions. Sometimes that decision was different from the recommendations of his officers, but it was always right.

After returning from Socoh with David and Joab, Ziba had found more time to think. And the more he thought, the more he compared David with Saul. Where David exuded confidence and reminded his men that they were fighting for the Lord God, Saul sat in darkness, unsure of himself and only willing to talk about God when someone else brought up His name. David was a victor, and not only in battle. Saul was already defeated.

Where Jonathan fit in all this, Ziba didn't understand. Jonathan and David were closer than ever before, and Ziba had put away his jealousy. He saw that Michal was with the man she was suited for. Now that he was a little more objective, Ziba saw that he could have never kept the spoiled princess satisfied. David, on the other hand, had a way about him that got Michal's attention and gave him mastery over his wife.

And that left Mara. Ziba was still perplexed at her behavior when

See 1 Samuel 19

they met on the staircase. And he was even more confused about why she left. If she truly was in love with him, why didn't she stay? *Men are a lot easier to understand*, he thought. *On the battlefield, a man said what he needed, and others provided it for him. Women never tell you what they need or want. They seem to want you to read their minds—something I am unwilling and unable to do.*

He sighed and shook his head. He watched David pass him in the hall. For once, David seemed very tired. Dust caked his shoulders and the tops of his feet. A fine powder covered his forehead, settling on his eyebrows and the tips of his lashes.

David passed the open door to the counting room, and Ziba heard Jonathan's voice. David stopped and went in. Jonathan had already told Ziba that there were no secrets between them, so curiosity got the better of Ziba. He followed David in the door. Jonathan nodded to Ziba, indicating that it was OK for Ziba to be there.

"David, I have just come from the throne room," Jonathan said. "Father is in one of his rages again. He has asked two other men and me to kill you."

David smiled thinly. "So, are you going to kill me?"

"Of course not," Jonathan said. "But this is an order from the king. It's not to be taken lightly."

"So what do you want to do?"

"You need to leave. Now."

David shook his head. "Nonsense. The king may have his moments, but he isn't likely to kill me. I win too many battles for him. I think you're overreacting."

Jonathan shook his head.

"I've never seen him like this. Look, just go. Head over to Samuel's country. He'll help you. And my father will hesitate to follow."

"No," David said. "It's just a passing rage. He gets them all the time."

"Tell you what. Tomorrow I'll take my father hunting in the field south of Gibeah. Do you know where the stream runs through there? Wait nearby. I'll talk to my father then come tell you what he says."

Years ago, before they were royalty, a father and son going hunting would be a solitary affair, giving them an opportunity to talk about personal things without being overheard. But being king and crown prince had taught Saul and Jonathan that the concept of privacy was a luxury they could no longer afford. Even though David had made the world safer for Israel by defeating many of the enemies that lived around them, there were always people—Israelites and others—who would take advantage of their being alone to try to kill them.

And so it was that Jonathan and Saul were alone—except for the two bodyguards who accompanied them. In this case, it was Ziba and his father, Achim, two people whom Saul and Jonathan could trust to keep what they said private. It was as solitary as the king and his son could get these days.

Jonathan and the king were hunting quail. Saul had been somewhat reluctant to go, but Ziba saw him relax as they left the palace and entered the wild. While Ziba and Achim moved forward and to one side to shake the brush with sticks, Jonathan and Saul stood ready with bows. Ziba could overhear them in the stillness, even though he was several feet away.

"Father," Jonathan said. "I want to talk to you about David." Ziba heard Saul sigh, and Ziba knew that this wouldn't be an easy discussion.

"Don't you think you've been unfair to him?" Jonathan asked.

Saul looked sharply at his son. "No, I don't. David is a menace to the throne."

"How can you say that, Father? Remember what it was like when Goliath was threatening us? How you worried that you would lose your army, and after that, your crown? If David wanted you off the throne, why did he risk his life to face the giant? How has he threatened us?"

Saul grumbled, but Ziba could see that he was softening. When he didn't answer, Jonathan continued.

"Think about how many battles David has won for you since then. Think of how many enemies he's killed. Every one of those enemies wanted to take you off the throne. How can you say that David is a danger when he's removed so much danger? If it weren't for him, would you feel as comfortable coming out here today to hunt?"

Jonathan paused, and finally Saul opened his mouth to speak.

"I . . . I may have been rash," he said. "You're right. He's made our lives easier. I just have to ignore the things I hear in the palace."

"Promise me, Father," Jonathan said. "Promise me that you won't kill David."

Saul thought for a moment, then nodded. "I swear to you in front of God, I won't kill David."

Ziba looked over toward the ravine where he knew David was hiding. Jonathan would go to him as soon as their hunting was over. He was safe for now. But for how long, no one could tell.

Even though David was a mighty man on the battlefield, even though he had thousands of soldiers who answered to him, Saul never forgot that David was a musician as well. Occasionally, when David was in the palace, Saul asked for David to come and sing to him. David seemed to welcome the opportunity, both to try to develop a relationship with Saul and because it reminded him of simpler times when his only audience was a flock of sheep and the stars above him in the sky.

Today, it was Abner who had requested that David come and sing. Saul was in a particularly troubled mood. He was so bad that no one could get him to respond. Instead, he sat on his throne staring straight ahead, oblivious to everyone and everything around him.

Rumor was that David and Michal were having a baby. Michal had been so concerned about her appearance that Ziba had wondered how she would respond to being with child, but he didn't have to worry. Whether it was true or not, Michal embraced her new status. Ziba thought it was because she would have someone small to take care of—and because she loved David so much. Their passionate love was accepted by everyone around them and was especially obvious to Ziba, who still longed for Michal to look at him that way. Rationally he knew it would never happen, but emotionally he'd never given up hope.

But today the rumor mill was buzzing. Even though David was playing and singing, Ziba could still hear people talking in the hallway and in the foyer outside the throne room.

"I wonder what they'll name the baby," someone was saying. "I wonder whether it will be a boy or a girl."

"It had better be a boy," someone else said. "Then when David takes the throne, no one will have any doubt that he'll have a successor." Their voices were clear enough that everyone in the throne room could hear them.

Stupid fools. Ziba looked toward the entrance, then toward the throne where Saul sat. Once again, he saw a dark cloud come over his face, and his knuckles grew white as he clenched the shaft of his spear. Off to one side in the alcove, out of sight of the king's audience, David sat singing:

"I lie down and sleep;
 I wake again, because the LORD sustains me.
I will not fear though tens of thousands
 assail me on every side."*

Ziba watched Saul's face as David sang. He could almost see the wheels turning as the king faced the front and stared at nothing in particular. And then he knew what would happen. Ziba started running.

An instant later, Saul stood quickly, spear in hand, and hefted it above his head. A half second after that, it was flying toward David. Ziba heard the spear crash into the wall. Others ran to the king, but Ziba ran toward David. When he reached the alcove, the curtain was ripped and the spear was embedded in the wall, but David was nowhere to be seen. Once again, he'd eluded death.

"Ziba!" he heard the king call behind him. Ziba turned.

"Yes, Your Majesty."

"Abner is forming a party to take David prisoner. Go with him. I know I can trust you."

"Yes, Your Majesty," Ziba said. Take him prisoner, the king had said, but Ziba knew better. Their job was to kill David, if they could.

They searched the palace for David, but he wasn't there. Michal wasn't there either.

---

* See Psalm 3:5, 6, NIV.

"David likes to stay at a house just out of town," Abner said. "It was given to him by an old shepherd. I know Michal has gone out there with him as well."

Ziba cleared his throat. "I've been in battle with this man before. I've seen him kill two hundred Philistines. He's not to be taken lightly."

Abner looked at Ziba and then nodded. "We'll surround the house so he can't go anywhere. Then when it gets light, we'll go in and get him."

"Abner," Ziba said. "Saul did say to capture David, didn't he?"

Abner stared at Ziba before responding. "Unpredictable things happen in battle."

Ziba knew how to translate that. Unless David came up with a miracle, he was a dead man.

Hiding behind a tree in the dark, Ziba could hear muffled voices coming from the house. One he recognized as Michal's, and he suspected the other one was David's. He was far enough away that he couldn't make out what they were saying. But their voices weren't as loud as the voices in his head.

It's another opportunity, a voice told him. *By tomorrow, David will either be dead or on the run. Michal will be lonely without her husband. You can comfort her.*

No, another voice said. *You had your opportunity for a meaningful relationship. But it wasn't with Michal. You had someone who loved you, and you threw it away. You don't deserve Mara, and you definitely don't deserve Michal.*

He tried to dismiss the voices, but they returned again and again. Finally, he settled into his post outside the house, eager for the morning. It would be a long night with only the crickets, the stars, and the voices in his head to keep him company.

Morning came, and as the light crept over the hills, Ziba saw Abner wave for the group to move forward. The moment of dawn provided enough light for them to see, and it was often the time when people were just waking up. In addition, with enough planning, the morning light would be in the victim's eyes. It was the perfect time to attack.

The house had two windows, one on either side, as well as a doorway. It was built on the edge of a cliff with the idea that sheep could be held in a small ravine on the other side. Ziba manned one window, with a second soldier at the other window. Abner and three other men prepared to rush the door.

Finally, Abner nodded, and the four men crashed through the door, swords held high. Ziba heard Michal scream. He peeked over the edge of the window and saw her standing in the corner, facing the doorway, her face white.

"What are you doing?" she shouted at Abner. "What gives you the right to break into my house?"

"The king's orders give me the right," Abner said. "Now where is David?"

Michal paused, and Ziba could tell that she was thinking quickly.

"He has a fever. Don't disturb him. I don't want the disease to spread."

Abner shook his head and didn't hesitate but crashed through the doorway into the second room. Inside was a bed with a still form beneath the covers, with only the top of his head showing.

"Maybe he *is* contagious," one of the soldiers said. "Maybe we should leave him alone."

Abner growled and pulled back the covers. Beneath them lay a wooden idol, one of those that presumably had been destroyed by Samuel years before. At the top, where the head should be, Michal had placed goats' hair instead of human hair.

"Where is he?" Abner repeated, a growl in his voice.

Michal broke into tears, and Ziba immediately knew that she was faking. Michal could be a great actress when the situation called for it, but Ziba had been around her enough to know what was real and what wasn't.

"He threatened to kill me unless I let him go," Michal said. "And I'm sure you wouldn't want the king's daughter killed, Abner. Would you?"

Abner grumbled to himself and stomped out the door, his soldiers close behind him. Ziba stood at the window. When he caught Michal's eye, he saw a glint of amusement come into them. Then she tipped her head slightly to point out something that Abner hadn't noticed.

Beneath a third window, facing the ravine, was a knotted rope. It was just long enough for someone to climb out the window and down into the ravine in the dead of night.

Chapter 15

Farewell

Jonathan and Ziba had to wait quite a while before they could check on David. Saul knew that Jonathan and David were close, and so he had his reliable staff, including Abner himself, watch Jonathan and Michal closely. Even Ziba, who still served as a messenger, was watched and debriefed every time he returned to the palace.

Ziba knew that Jonathan was waiting for the king's attitude to mellow, as he knew it would. Just as Saul could be instantly filled with rage, that rage would disappear over time, leaving Saul to wonder what had happened not too long afterward. It was as if someone else lived inside his body and chose certain moments to come out and attack anyone and everyone around him.

But after a few months, Ziba saw a difference in Saul. His rages ceased, and instead, he began settling into another depression. And then he began asking for David.

"It would be wonderful to hear his voice again," Saul said one day in the throne room. "I miss hearing him sing and play."

Jonathan only nodded, looking over Saul's shoulder at Ziba.

"Why don't you ask him to come and play for me? Or has he gone on one of his missions?"

Jonathan cleared his throat. "He's gone, Father. Remember, you threw your spear at him?"

Saul stared at Jonathan as if struggling to remember who his son was. Then he nodded.

See 1 Samuel 20

"I don't remember doing that, but if you say I did, then it probably happened," Saul said. "I may have done a foolish thing. All that I know is that I miss him and would like to see him again."

Jonathan looked at Ziba, who raised an eyebrow but said nothing.

Ziba expected the king to forget about David, but he didn't. For several months he continued to ask about his former champion. Finally, Jonathan pulled Ziba aside and talked to him.

"What do you think? Is the king serious about wanting David back? Can I trust him?"

Ziba shrugged. "You know him better than anyone. What does your heart tell you?"

Jonathan looked down. "My heart tells me that I miss David as well. Father is unpredictable. Lately, his rages have disappeared. It's enough to give me hope."

"Hope is one thing. A practical prediction is another. Is there any guarantee that Saul won't fall into one of his rages again?"

Jonathan sadly shook his head. "With Father, there are no guarantees of anything. Hope is all I have."

"What do you want to do? Do you want me to go look for David?"

Jonathan shook his head. "I already know where he is. He's in Naioth, near Ramah. He's close enough to Samuel that the prophet can help keep him safe. He's got about one hundred men there too. Father sent a company of men to capture David, but they came back singing and praising God, forgetting why the king sent them down in the first place."

Ziba stared at him and shook his head. "With any other person, that would be surprising news. With David, it's more of the usual thing."

"David does have the ability to make the ordinary into the extraordinary," Jonathan said. "That's what makes him special. That, and having a very special relationship with our God." He looked into Ziba's eyes and slapped him on the shoulder. "You and I are going to ride down to Naioth and see our friend David."

Ziba nodded. It was risky with Saul's men following their every move, but there was risk in everything they did these days.

❧

A week later, Ziba accompanied Jonathan into a field outside the town of Naioth. Knowing that Saul's men were watching the stables closely, Ziba and Jonathan traveled on foot. One of David's men stopped them before they ever got to the town. When they explained who they were and what they wanted, the young man told them to meet David under a tamarisk tree that stood nearby. A few minutes later, David stepped out of the shadows. Ziba saw that David moved with the same stealth he'd used in Socoh several years before.

Jonathan and David embraced, and David nodded to acknowledge Ziba as well.

"It's good to see you, my friend," Jonathan said. "You are missed."

"You two look well," David said. "How are things in the palace?"

Jonathan looked at Ziba, then smiled at David. "Father is asking for you. He wants you to come and play for him again."

David stared at Jonathan, then at Ziba. "You can't be serious."

Jonathan nodded. "I'm serious. Father has settled down. He's a lot calmer than before. Look, I can't promise anything, but I think that it's OK."

David shook his head and looked at the ground.

"It's not your head at risk here," David said. "I've tried and tried to please your father. I killed a giant for him. I've fought and won countless battles for him. I've killed his enemies. And how does he repay me? He orders his son—my best friend—to kill me. And when that doesn't work, he throws a spear at me. He wants me dead, that's for sure."

"I won't let that happen. That's a promise." Jonathan reached out and put his hand on David's shoulder, who still looked unconvinced.

"I swear to you with God as my witness," Jonathan said. "I make a pact that I'll always protect you and your household. Forever. And I'm asking you to promise the same thing."

"I could never hurt you, Jonathan. You and yours will always be safe as long as I'm around." David put his hand on Jonathan's shoulder in return. "I promise.

"The Festival of the New Moon is tomorrow. I'll wait in that field where we met a year ago, and you can test your father's sincerity regarding me. If you're still convinced that he's safe, I'll return with you. If not, we'll say goodbye."

Jonathan nodded, "That's fair enough," he said.

The Festival of the New Moon was one of the biggest festivals of the year. Everyone but the essential servants had the day off as part of the celebration. King Saul was in good spirits and took his place at the head of the great table, with Abner seated off to the right. Servants brought fresh fruit, mutton on the bone, and many delicacies, including some of Saul's favorites. Jonathan took his seat opposite the king and picked at his food. He tried to be cheerful but was having a hard time finding enough to be cheerful about. On the second night, King Saul commented on Jonathan's solemn demeanor.

"Oh come on, Jonathan," Saul said. "Why the long face? There's a lot to be thankful for. We have peace in our land, something I never thought I'd see. We have a bountiful crop. Abner even tells me that we've rounded up and killed every witch within our borders. Every one." He turned and looked at Abner, who nodded.

"And you have one person to thank for having a peaceful land," Jonathan said quietly. "David, son of Jesse."

Saul stared at Jonathan as if hearing the name for the very first time.

"And where is David, son of Jesse? Shouldn't he be here? What, is he sick? Why wasn't I informed?"

Jonathan looked at Abner, who looked confused. Neither knew how to answer the king. Finally Jonathan answered.

"Uh, David has urgent business at home in Bethlehem. I gave him permission to ride down there."

Ziba saw Saul's face cloud up and change within seconds. One moment he was cheerful and happy. A second later, the familiar rage had taken over his face and body.

"You son of a whore," Saul said, standing. The room was suddenly silent. "You think I don't know that you've sided with David against me? You're all plotting to take me from the throne. Don't you know that as long as David is alive, you'll never be king? You shame me. You shame your mother. You shame yourself!"

"Father, why are you so obsessed with killing David?" Jonathan said, standing as well. "What has he done to deserve execution? Everything he's done has been for you. He's won battle after battle for you. This peace you speak of exists because of him. *Do you even know what you're doing?*" His words ended in a shout.

Saul's face reddened and then almost turned purple. Ziba thought Saul's head would explode. Then the rage took over. In an instant, Saul had raised his spear and launched it at Jonathan. Ziba had just enough time to reach out and grab Jonathan by the arm, pulling him away from the flight of the spear.

The feast was over as both Jonathan and Saul were hustled from the room. The night had been a disaster, but at least Jonathan and David had their answer.

Ziba accompanied a very sober Jonathan and his small son, Jethro, to the field where they had agreed to meet David. Jonathan had told his son that they would be testing a new bow, and he had the job of fetching the arrows. Jonathan shot two arrows into the air. They landed at the far end of the field. When Jethro had left, Jonathan turned to Ziba.

"You're my best friend," he said. "But this is a conversation that David and I need to have alone. Very likely, this will be the last time we'll see each other."

Ziba nodded. He'd anticipated such a request from Jonathan, and even though he now knew that Jonathan was truly his best friend, the prince had a special bond with David. He dreaded the idea of having to say goodbye to Jonathan, and so he understood.

Ziba turned and headed to the small hill between the field and the town of Gibeah, thinking about Mara the whole way. He was a warrior, unafraid of anything on the battlefield. He was battle tested, having accompanied both Jonathan and David on their adventures. He was bold and adventurous. So what was it that made him grow frightened when he thought of Mara? He'd long thought that he wanted Michal, but he now knew that what he felt for Michal was only a shallow taste of what love is. And as he thought about it, he realized that he was in love with Mara. She'd been in his mind every moment since she left Gibeah.

The problem was, he'd heard that she'd already gotten married in Jabesh-gilead. Her husband was a young, but successful, farmer who already had two sons but had lost his first wife. Ziba hoped she was happy but saw no reason to go to Jabesh-gilead anymore.

He saw Jethro returning to Jonathan with the arrows.

"You missed one," Jonathan said. "There was a third one that I shot. Go a little farther." Obedient but mystified, Jethro turned and ran across the field, away from Jonathan.

When Jethro was gone, Ziba saw David step from the ravine and into the dry grass of the field. He slowly approached Jonathan. Ziba could hear Jonathan's low voice but couldn't hear words. He could tell that Jonathan was visibly upset. As Ziba watched, Jonathan slumped over and began to cry. David stepped forward and put his arms around his friend. Ziba felt for Jonathan and fought back tears himself. They stood there for a long time, their arms around each other. Finally David stepped back and said something to Jonathan that sounded like words of reassurance. Jonathan nodded to David. They then clasped hands and hugged one more time. David took a deep breath and turned to reenter the ravine. A moment after he'd disappeared, Jethro reappeared. The boy held up his hands as if he couldn't find the arrow, an arrow that didn't exist.

"It's all right, son," Jonathan shouted, the words choking in his voice. "Come back. It's time to go home."

Ziba walked down the hill to meet Jonathan and Jethro. At first, no one said anything. Jethro, acting like the eight-year-old boy that he was, ran and danced around Ziba's feet. Jonathan walked with his head down, with Ziba following.

After a while, Ziba got up the courage to speak.

"You'll see him again," he said.

"No, I won't," Jonathan said. "This is the end. He'll be king, and I'll be wherever God plans for me to be. But it doesn't matter. We're brothers. We're bonded. We made a pact. I'll always honor his children, just as he'll honor mine.

"It's the best thing to do. It's the only thing to do."

Chapter 16

The Witch of Endor

The man in the dark cloak and hood watched as Zephan closed her eyes and began muttering incoherently. After a few moments, it was as if the walls of the dark, small cottage were beginning to collapse in on the two of them. Then all of a sudden, they stood in a bright meadow with sunshine warming their shoulders. Birds twittered in the trees above them, and the man could see a deer walking out of the trees some distance away.

"Remarkable," was all that he could say. "We're not really there, are we?"

"No," Zephan replied. "But your mind thinks we are. And if the mind believes it, how is it not real?" She waved her hands, and the room returned to darkness.

"But how?" The man threw back his hood, revealing that he was King Achish of Gath. He was older now, with gray hair and lines on his face. His belly was round, and it rolled when he walked. Zephan looked almost the same as she had more than thirty years before, and Achish wondered how much of it was witchcraft.

Zephan smiled. Her teeth showed white in the light of the fireplace.

"As I said, it's all in the mind. Your sorcerers were right. Once I let go of my old beliefs, there was a mighty leap in what I could do."

"And what beliefs were those?"

"The belief that the Hebrew God is all-powerful." She stepped toward the old king, her eyes narrowing. "I've discovered that there is

See 1 Samuel 28

power in the darkness as well. Giving myself to it has made all the difference."

Achish smiled. "Then we're almost ready. After all these years, I think I've discovered the way to beat Israel."

"What's changed?"

"Saul has become obsessed with tracking down and killing his nemesis, David. David and I have reached an agreement, and he and his men now live with me. I've found him very helpful in ridding me of my troublesome enemies."

Zephan raised an eyebrow. "But I thought David had sworn an oath not to attack Saul."

Achish nodded. "That doesn't mean he won't attack all our other enemies. Moabites, Amalekites—yes, they're still around—even the Egyptians when they come too far north. With him there, I kill three birds with one stone. He rids me of annoying enemies, he frees up my army to raise havoc with Israel, and he continues to vex King Saul."

"You're very wise, my king."

"That's just the beginning," Achish said, continuing. "And that's where you come in. I wouldn't be here—sneaking into Israel in the middle of the night—if it weren't so. Saul is falling apart, from the inside out. And with him, the nation of Israel is collapsing as well. I'll provide a well-placed attack, and you'll do the rest."

"Me? What can I do?"

"You, my beautiful, wicked sorceress, will remove all hope from the king of Israel. I'll destroy him from without. You'll destroy him from within."

As low as the nation seemed to be when David left Jonathan, nine years of emotional famine had followed. Saul seemed to crumble before their eyes. Jonathan continued to take care of domestic issues, and Abner continued to run the army. Israel had very few enemies now, thanks to David, but as time wore on, the diminished nations around them began to grow again. Abner sought no approval or disapproval from Saul for his actions, and Ziba knew that he wouldn't get either one from Saul anyway. In the meantime, Jonathan was grateful for Abner's willingness to take on that responsibility.

But that didn't mean there weren't internal struggles as well. Even with the unity that had come with the Battle of Michmash, Jonathan's notoriety throughout the kingdom, and the marriage to Rahab that followed, the nation was beginning to fragment. Even a third child, the baby Mephibosheth, didn't seem to make much difference to the northern tribes. Judah and Benjamin in the south were faithful in following King Saul, while the ten tribes to the north began making decisions on their own.

Once again, Ziba lost contact with Jonathan, but this time instead of David, Ziba was competing with the overwhelming work that faced Jonathan. He worked by lamplight from early in the morning before the sun came up until late at night. And still, not everything got done. Every day Ziba saw roads that needed mending, bridges that were collapsing, and whole villages that had been abandoned.

Just when he thought it couldn't get any worse, it did. News began arriving of a new force of Philistines mustering in the south. It was time to once again call on the army of Israel to defend their homeland. But that issue was never in more question than today.

Ziba returned to the counting room after another trip to the north, this time to collect news from Jonathan's father-in-law, Hirt. Ziba stood in front of Jonathan's desk for several minutes while Jonathan continued with his nose buried in the scrolls that lay in front of him. Finally, Ziba cleared his throat, and Jonathan looked up. He smiled through a tired face, then stretched, his arms held over his head.

"Ziba," Jonathan said, "what's the news from the north? Is it as bad as I thought it might be?"

"Worse," Ziba said. "I'm sorry I can't bring better news. The northern tribes won't join the fight. They have another solution, one that you won't like."

"And what's that? That we talk them into surrender?"

"Pretty much. They want us to send an emissary to Gath and ask for a peace treaty. They basically want us to surrender."

Jonathan shook his head. "Achish wouldn't sign a peace treaty. You and I know him well enough for that. And even if he did, it wouldn't be worth the parchment it was printed on."

Ziba nodded. "So what's the plan?"

"Abner is still trying to rouse Father from his lethargy. If we can get him up and moving, there's still a chance we can collect enough men to hold our own against Achish."

Ziba followed Jonathan down the hall and into the throne room. Abner stood next to Saul, seated on his throne, talking to him quietly. Saul, as usual, stared straight ahead. His face was deeply lined, and he'd lost all color, his skin showing pale white in the light of the torches. His hair, white and long, lay scattered across his shoulders.

Jonathan approached the throne, and Abner turned and saw Jonathan and Ziba. He shook his head. Jonathan cleared his throat and stepped closer to his father.

"Father. Your Majesty. We need you badly. We need someone to lead us into battle. Once again the Philistines are invading. We need you."

Jonathan stopped, and they watched for a reaction from Saul. There was none. Jonathan looked back at Ziba.

"I have an idea, even though it might not sound that practical," Ziba said. "Let's pray."

Jonathan brightened. "That's not impractical at all. We'll pray with Father."

"Excuse me," Abner said. "I'll take your leave. I have work to do."

Jonathan and Ziba looked at each other as Abner walked out of the room. Ziba shook his head. He suspected they were both thinking the same thing, but neither one spoke it. Abner wasn't helping things, but this was not the time for dissension. They bowed their heads.

"Lord God, maker of heaven and earth," Jonathan began. "You were there when we climbed the cliffs of Michmash and fought the Philistines against overwhelming odds. You were there when we were faced by a brutal giant, and You sent us David to overcome our enemies. You've always been there. And now we ask that You help us one more time.

"We are again under siege. The Philistines want to destroy our land, our people. Give us the answer. Give us the power to respond."

Jonathan's prayer was interrupted by the raspy voice of Saul.

"He's not listening," Saul said. "God has cursed me, and now the whole nation is cursed. We're doomed to destruction."

"Father, that's not true," Jonathan said. "God forgives, always. He may have other plans for the throne, but there's still time to ask for forgiveness for your past and present sins and surrender to His love."

Saul turned his head and laughed quietly at Jonathan.

"Love? What does our God know of love? If He knew of love, I wouldn't be cursed. And I wouldn't have spent the last twenty years asking for forgiveness with no hope of finding it."

Jonathan looked at Ziba, then back at Saul.

"We need to come to Him with a sincere heart, Father," Jonathan said. "He *will* forgive, if we really, truly want forgiveness."

Saul exhaled and stretched. "There's no hope for me. But perhaps there's still hope for my kingdom." He looked down at Jonathan. "And my son. What did I do to deserve such a good son?"

Jonathan's eyes brightened.

"Then you'll rise up and call for our people to fight?" Jonathan asked.

Saul nodded, and color began to return to his cheeks. "It will be my last battle. I see that now. But I'll build us an army, and I'll lead them into battle, no matter what the outcome is."

Jonathan's face broke into a grin, and he turned and slapped Ziba on the shoulder.

"Come with me," Jonathan said. "We've got work to do."

"Jonathan," Ziba said as they hurried down the hallway, again pursuing a merchant for the funds to go to war. "Why do you follow your father? You could have gone with David when he left."

"Because I have family here. Because he's my father."

"It's not because you're still in line for the throne?"

"I've given up all hope of becoming king," Jonathan said. "It was never my wish to begin with. My wish has always been to serve God wherever He sends me. Whatever fate He has for me."

"But our king is mad. You know that, don't you?"

Jonathan turned and gave Ziba a sharp look. "He may be a little mad, but he's my father. I love him, whatever he does to me."

Ziba cleared his throat and hesitated. "Have you ever thought one day you might have to choose between God and your father?"

Jonathan looked at Ziba darkly. "I hope that day never comes. I've been fortunate so far." He reached out and clutched Ziba's shoulder. "Whatever happens, I'm pleased to have called you my friend."

Ziba smiled and nodded as he followed Jonathan down the hallway.

It took ten days to gather what might vaguely be described as an army. There was a core of soldiers who were currently fighting under Abner. They numbered about a thousand. Then there was a militia of veterans from previous campaigns, most beginning to show their age and a few with a hand or some other body part missing. During normal times, Jonathan would have turned them away to return to their homes. But they were in desperate straits. It was exactly opposite of the Battle of Michmash. They had plenty of weapons—now they needed men.

Jonathan and Ziba held their breath and prayed that Saul would remain in his right mind. Fortunately, Saul became more and more animated as time wore on. Abner, on the other hand, seemed distant and hardly talked to Jonathan, or even to King Saul. Ziba wondered if it was because he was discouraged by the turnout for his "army."

At the end of ten days, word came that the Philistines were on the march. Their army, led by five hundred chariots, was traveling up the coastal road to the north. Abner, Jonathan, and Saul agreed that the Philistine's plan was the same as all those years before. They would cut across the kingdom of Israel at Geba and try to cut the nation in half.

Saul and Abner took the lead of the column that left Gibeah and headed north, with Jonathan and his brothers Ishvi and Malki-Shua riding behind them. The armor-bearers and other bodyguards, including Ziba, Uthai, and Ziba's father, Achim, rode behind them. The youngest son of Saul, Eshbaal,* stayed at home—Saul insisted that at least one heir should remain behind in case things went badly.

The column hardly could be called that, thought Ziba. He'd been in many marches in many military situations. This collection of farmers,

---

* Later known as Ish-bosheth.

shepherds, and merchants bore no resemblance to an army marching. He turned and tried to make his thoughts brighter.

When they got to Geba, Ziba sighed with relief. Getting there a few days before the Philistines would give them that much time to train their "army." But just as soon as the old army compound came into sight, a rider came charging up in front of them. He pulled up his horse and dust flew everywhere.

"The Philistines are continuing north," the rider said to Saul. Saul and Abner looked at each other. Abner spoke.

"Then we have to continue north."

An hour later, it began to rain.

The rain didn't stop but got progressively worse as they marched farther north. The column strung out across a great distance, and Ziba and Jonathan were given the task of prompting stragglers to rejoin the marching army. When they got to Bethel, Abner decided to give the army a rest. While their men sat in the rain, Abner, Saul, and Jonathan found a home where they could get a warm drink and discuss the direction the Philistines could have gone. As usual, Ziba tagged along.

"I still think they mean to cut us in two," said Abner. "But where?"

"There are two more passes across the mountains," Jonathan said. "They could be crossing at Shechem, or farther north at Jezreel. I don't really understand the logic at either one. Michmash is a lot more strategic."

"Perhaps their plan isn't to cut our country in half," Saul said slowly. "Perhaps they simply want to destroy our army."

Abner nodded. "Making us march so far in driving rain and little time to rest would do it. We'll be worn out by the time we get where we're going—wherever that is."

Jonathan frowned. "Father, I recommend that we send scouts out to determine where the Philistines will be."

Ziba raised his hand. "I know every road between here and Dan. I volunteer."

Jonathan smiled and put his hand on Ziba's shoulder. Then he turned to his father. There was no response from the king, and Jonathan saw that he was rapidly approaching another one of his depressions.

"Choose two other riders, Ziba," Jonathan said. "When you're done, try to catch up with us on our way north. You shouldn't have any problem, considering how slow our column is."

Ziba sent one scout to Shechem and the road that traveled west from there. He sent the second one to Jezreel, farther north. He decided to ride straight west and try to catch the rear of the Philistine column.

A day later, Ziba was back. He was covered with mud, and his horse was exhausted. The column had made better time than they had anticipated. Ziba had to ride back to Bethel and then north. He caught the last of the column just south of Jezreel, still traveling in the driving rain.

"So you heard," Ziba said to Jonathan when he entered the tent that had been set up in Jezreel. Ziba noticed a tray filled with bowls of hot broth, and he greedily picked up one and put it to his lips.

"We heard that the Philistines were headed east from the coast, but not how many or what kind of armaments. How bad is it?" Jonathan asked.

"Bad," Ziba said. "I talked to Israelites settled on the coast road. They told me of a mass of infantry, cavalry, archers, and about five hundred chariots. I estimate a total force of about fifteen thousand."

"And they're all trained killers," Jonathan said, mostly to himself. "Not shepherds."

"I knew a shepherd once who killed a giant," Ziba said. "It can be done. With Jehovah on our side, it can be done."

Jonathan turned, smiled, and nodded. "Thanks for reminding me, Ziba. Now get some dry clothes and something to eat."

When Abner and Saul returned from their inspection of the army and its bivouac, Jonathan told them what Ziba had said. Abner looked down and muttered some strange oath, but Saul said nothing. Ziba looked at Saul and saw nothing behind his eyes. *The man is dead and doesn't know it yet*, he thought.

"The rain may help us," Jonathan said. "It'll bog down their chariots."

"What we need is a high place," said Abner, turning to the map on the table. "Rocky to protect us from their archers and cavalry. Here," he said, pointing at a place on the map. "Mount Gilboa. We can position ourselves on the slope. We'll have the advantage of higher ground, rocky outcroppings, and a location where we can't be outflanked."

"It's better than open field," Jonathan said, nodding.

Jonathan left the tent to check on the horses, but Ziba went and sat on a pile of baggage in the corner, still trying to dry off and warm up. Apparently the other two didn't see him there, and when he heard their conversation, he understood why they wanted privacy.

"Abner," Saul began. "You killed all the witches in the kingdom, didn't you?"

Abner paused, then nodded. "Yes, Your Majesty. Upon your order."

Saul stared at him. "That's a shame. I really need to talk to Samuel now."

Abner raised an eyebrow. "Samuel is dead, Your Majesty. He's been dead for years."

"But I've heard that witches have great power. Even power to contact the dead. Are you sure there are no witches left?"

Abner paused, and Ziba could tell that he was trying to protect himself.

"There is one witch. In Endor. I've heard that she's very powerful."

Saul looked into Abner's eyes, and once again, all Ziba could see was a dead man.

"Take me to her," Saul said.

Chapter 17

The Last Battle

Ziba couldn't believe his ears. From the time that he was a child, he'd been taught to avoid witches at all costs. For Saul to ask to visit a witch to talk to someone who'd been dead for years, well, that was unheard of. He waited until Saul and Abner had left the tent, then crept out himself.

Jonathan had spent time with the horses, checking to make sure they were in good shape for the battle. He'd left there and was talking to soldiers huddled around a campfire when Ziba arrived.

"We need to talk—*now!*" Ziba hissed, and Jonathan followed him away from the fire. Ziba told Jonathan what he'd heard.

Jonathan shook his head. "The demon that my father has been struggling with for years has finally taken over. He's totally given up on God."

"He's desperate," Ziba said.

"He's insane," Jonathan answered. "He's desperate to talk to Samuel, to somehow get his blessing."

"But Samuel's dead," Ziba said. "How . . . ?"

"He's not going to be talking to Samuel. He'll be talking to whomever, or whatever, this witch conjures up. Ziba, this can't continue."

Ziba bit his lip and stared at the ground.

"Abner told him that all witches were killed. Then he tells him tonight there is still one around. A powerful one. In Endor."

Jonathan took a breath. "Abner's mother, Zephan, lives in Endor."

See 1 Samuel 28 and 31

"She's always been a little strange. In fact, I've heard rumors that she's visited Gath once or twice."

"You don't think . . . ?" Jonathan said. "If Abner knew about her, then maybe he's in on something."

"I've suspected him of ill will ever since we were kids before Jabesh-gilead," Ziba said.

"Ziba, we'll deal with him later. On the battlefield. But you have to stop the king from visiting that woman."

"How do I stop him? He *is* a king, after all."

Jonathan turned back toward the fire. "If you can get there before him, kill her. She's under a death penalty, after all." His face grew hard. "And if you're too late, kill her anyway."

Ziba nodded and turned to leave.

"But first there's something else I need you to do," Jonathan said. "Something I've worried about for a long time."

Army camps don't vary a lot in appearance, especially in the dead of night. The rain had stopped, but it was cold. Men stood around campfires trying to get warm. Others warmed up food and tried to eat. There were clumps of clothing here and there, with soldiers trying to sleep for a few hours—or a few minutes.

Ziba thought about this as he crept through the Philistine camp. Dressed like the other camp followers, many of them Israelites from the north, Ziba had no trouble entering the camp of his enemy. They had searched him for weapons, and he'd wisely left his armor and sword behind. Instead, he wore only rough clothes that a farmer or poor merchant would wear.

He strode through the camp, looking for the section cordoned off for David and his men. When he found it, David was standing next to Joab, warming himself by the campfire. He was dressed in leathers, just as he had been years ago when Ziba had followed him to Socoh. His face was lined and dirty, but he still had a boyish look about him, one that Ziba knew women would always be attracted to.

Ziba walked briskly across the open space toward David, when a soldier suddenly appeared and drew his sword and pointed it at Ziba's chest.

"That's OK, Abiezer," David said, looking up. "I know him."

Abiezer sheathed his sword, and Ziba stepped forward.

"Ziba," David said casually, reaching out his hand to shake Ziba's. "It's good to see you."

"I wish it were under better circumstances," Ziba said, out of breath. "Jonathan sent me."

"Jonathan! How goes it with Jonathan?" David asked, suddenly very intent on the answer.

"He's here, preparing for battle," Ziba said.

"I thought Saul would never let him return to battle."

"Things have disintegrated since you were last in Gibeah," Ziba said. "Saul is a shell of a man, and Jonathan felt he had to be there to lead."

David's face grew hard. "He's going to be killed."

Ziba nodded. "He's already accepted that. He just doesn't want to face you in battle."

David turned and faced Ziba, the hard look still on his face.

"And I don't want to face him. But I can't just leave. Achish would stop me and my men."

Joab stepped forward. "I'm friends with Gerar, Achish's second in command. Let me tell him that we're reluctant to fight our own people. I'll remind him of what happened at Michmash, where the Israelites turned against the Philistines in mid-battle."

David nodded. "That should do it." He turned back to Ziba. "Tell Jonathan not to worry. I won't fight him."

"There's one more thing," Ziba said. "Abner has betrayed us. He's been helping the Philistines from the beginning. If he survives the battle, I need you to kill him."

David shook his head. "I won't raise my hand against another Israelite. I've already sworn this." He stepped away from the fire and disappeared into the darkness.

Ziba started to leave, but Joab grabbed his arm.

"I've made no such oath," he told Ziba. "A traitor is a traitor, and they all must be killed. Leave it to me."

Ziba nodded, and Joab continued.

"But you need to get out of here. It's miles to Jezreel, and it'll be light soon. You'd better hurry."

"I'm not headed to Jezreel," Ziba said. "I'm going to Endor."

The Philistine camp was on the road to Endor, but the stop made Ziba doubt that he could get to the witch's home before Saul and Abner. He suspected Jonathan had thought the same thing. But telling David to stay out of the battle had been important to Jonathan, more important than saving a king who'd already decided to kill himself, one way or another.

Ziba pushed his horse as fast as he dared. The sun was coming up by the time he arrived at Endor. He asked a few people where the home of Zephan was. By their frightened expressions, he knew they were telling the truth.

He rode on to the other side of town and found a small, isolated house. All sense of propriety was tossed aside; this was not a social call. He was here to kill the woman, one way or another.

He kicked the door down.

Zephan stood facing the fireplace and didn't turn toward him even when the crash of the door splintering filled the room. He could see that she'd been a beautiful young girl once. Now she was just a tired old woman.

"You're too late," she said. "Saul has met Samuel. The prophet told him what he already knew; that Saul was doomed to die on the battlefield."

"You and I know that wasn't Samuel he talked to," Ziba said. "And I find it hard to believe that you would let your son Abner go to his death on the battlefield if we're all doomed. You're smarter than that."

"Ah, yes, Abner," Zephan said. "He's finally chosen the right side to be on. You won't see him on the battlefield. He's returned to Gibeah."

Ziba narrowed his eyes. "Then that makes my job simpler. All I have to do is kill you."

He drew a sword that David had given him and charged forward. Zephan deftly moved to the side, and Ziba missed. As Ziba turned to attack again, he blinked and saw that Zephan was standing on the rafters high above his head. He picked up a knife from the table and threw it at her.

The witch disappeared again and stood by the doorway.

"Run, if you want to," Ziba said. "I'm not too old to run you down. And when I catch you, I'll kill you."

The witch raised her arms, and everything changed. Instead of standing in a dark house, Ziba was standing by the fountain in the garden of Gibeah. It was so real he had a hard time remembering where he was. The birds twittered in the trees above his head, and he heard the sound of rippling water. Across from him on the patio stood not a witch but Michal.

"Oh Ziba," Michal said, stepping forward. "You've come back to me. At last, you're mine and mine alone."

Again, it was a struggle to remember that he was in Endor, not Gibeah. And who or what he faced was not Michal. Ziba stared at the image for a moment, then spoke.

"I'm sorry to disappoint you, Michal," he said. "But I love someone else."

With those words, he drove the sword he held into the belly of the image of Michal, an image that turned back into the witch.

Ziba arrived at the campsite for Israel by late morning. His horse was exhausted and frothing at the mouth. He was in a hurry to get back to the army before the battle began, but he knew it was another ten miles to Mount Gilboa. He rested his horse, all the time searching the abandoned camp for another horse, a donkey, or a camel that might have been left behind.

After about thirty minutes, Ziba felt he couldn't wait any longer. He mounted his horse and galloped eastward, hoping he could catch up with the army. Two miles down the road, his horse collapsed.

Muttering to himself, he looked at the exhausted horse, lying on its side. He knew that it would never rise again. He pulled out his sword and slashed its throat. Then he ran down the road to the east.

The sky was black with arrows. A few came from the cluster of archers that huddled behind the armored front line of the Israelites. Many more of them came from the Philistine line below them.

Uthai stood to the side of Saul and Jonathan, staring at the enemy below. Whereas Israel's army struggled to provide a straight battle line, the Philistine army was obviously disciplined and well trained.

"See that?" Achim said to Uthai, pointing to a black banner to the side with a white inscription on it. "Those are Hittites. I've heard of them but never seen them. They're not supposed to be this far south."

"I guess Achish's money can buy lots of things," Uthai said. "Including armor, weapons, and soldiers."

"Cover!" came the command again, and Uthai threw up his shield just in time to protect himself from a hail of black arrows. Many around them were not as quick and not as fortunate. Uthai heard screams all around him.

"Here come the chariots," muttered someone. It was followed by a general command: "Chariots!"

Uthai felt rather than heard the rumble of a hundred chariots coming up the hillside. They had chosen the spot because they believed the rocks above would shelter them from the arrows, and the rocks around them would stop the chariots, somewhat leveling the playing field. But they soon learned that the rocky ground was smooth enough for the chariots to run and made for solid ground as opposed to the mud that surrounded them. By the time they had arrived at their chosen spot, it was too late to move. The Philistines were upon them within fifteen minutes.

Uthai saw Jonathan turn to his father.

"Those chariots will rip us to shreds," he said to Saul. "Our forces know that. They'll scatter unless someone goes down there to help steady the line."

Saul shook his head. "I won't sacrifice you. Today or ever."

"Will you sacrifice your army? Will you sacrifice your kingdom? You should have thought of that last night when you saw that witch mother of Abner's. By the way, where is Abner?"

Saul said nothing, but Jonathan continued, his voice getting louder by the minute.

"I won't stand by and do nothing while our army is crushed," he shouted at Saul and then turned and ran down the hill toward the front line.

"He's a courageous man," Uthai said.

Achim sighed. "He's a dead man. But then, we're all dead, aren't we?" He looked down the slope at the carnage. "I'm just glad that Ziba isn't here."

"Speaking of not here, where's Abner?" Uthai asked. Achim didn't answer.

Uthai watched as Jonathan joined the front line, shouting to them even before he arrived.

"Courage, men! Yes, we are outnumbered, but we have God's angels fighting with us. Jehovah Himself is with us! Now straighten that line."

The few men on the line seemed to take courage from Jonathan's words, and for a brief moment, Uthai sensed a surge of confidence within them. Then the horns of battle blew again, and the confidence disappeared. A moment later, the first chariots appeared.

"Hold the line!" Jonathan said. "Spears at the ready! Archers, take out those drivers!" Jonathan had soldiers brace the shafts of long spears in the ground in hopes that the chariots' horses would impale themselves on them.

Arrows fired at the chariots, but it was too little, too late. Jonathan loosed arrow after arrow at the chariots. Some found their mark and men fell dead from the iron-bound wagons. But many others bounced off the sides of the chariots or the armor of the drivers.

The iron chariots charged through the line, cutting down the men as if they were grass. Jonathan dropped his bow, picked up a nearby spear, and threw it at the chariot that approached him. The spear pierced the iron armor and drove through the driver. Screaming in fright, the horses went one way while the chariot went the other. A second later, it was rolling right toward Jonathan. As Uthai and Achim watched in horror, the iron chariot rolled over the prince.

Uthai left his spot as armor-bearer and ran down the slope to the prince. He knew that Jonathan was dead even before he got to him.

He heard an order given: "Prepare for infantry."

What do they need infantry for? Uthai thought. *The chariots are enough to rip us to pieces.* He turned and hurried back to his place next to Saul.

Within ten minutes, it was obvious that not only would Israel lose the battle, but Achish intended to slaughter every Israelite on the field. Infantry marched forward to occupy the front line while Philistine cavalry and chariots destroyed Israelite cavalry. Arrows flew in all directions. Uthai turned to say something to Achim and saw him lying next to him, three arrows in his chest. *His death had come instantly*, Uthai thought. *But it was death all the same.*

He looked up at Saul, who must have been thinking the same thing. He turned to his young armor-bearer, who had recently replaced old Achim.

"Kill me," Saul blurted out to the boy.

"What? I can't kill you, Your Majesty." The boy shook his head.

"The battle is lost. I'm lost. God has abandoned us. Kill me." He turned from the boy to Uthai, who shook his head as well. *This is insanity*, Uthai thought. He looked into the wild eyes of the mad king. Then King Saul grabbed the sword of his armor-bearer and, before anyone could stop him, fell forward on it, impaling himself.

Uthai stared at the prone figure of the king, blood pooling on his armor and on the ground. The young armor-bearer, hardly more than a boy, looked at the king, then at Uthai.

"It was too quick," he stammered. "I couldn't stop him."

Uthai nodded and then heard a shout.

"Chariots!"

He heard a rumble behind him, and then all was blackness.

It was late afternoon by the time Ziba reached Mount Gilboa, and he immediately knew that he was too late. Smoke rose in many places, and scavengers—animal and human—skittered from body to body on the slope. He paused, catching his breath, and then ran up the slope. He knew that Saul—and Jonathan—would stand at the highest point on the slope, commanding the army from behind the center of the line. The rocky outcroppings that Abner had talked about were scattered here and there, but Ziba realized that there wasn't as much stone for protection as he'd promised.

He reached the top of the pile of bodies and found the banner that belonged to King Saul. A mass of bodies lay around it, and with dread in his heart, he looked for anyone he could recognize. He found the body of Achim.

"Father!" Ziba shouted, then fell to the ground next to the still form. Three arrows protruded from his chest.

"He was a brave man," Ziba heard behind him. "He stood by Saul to the very end." Ziba turned and saw a familiar figure.

"Uthai," Ziba said quietly, his words catching in his throat. "How is it that you survived?"

"Lucky, I guess," the man said, holding a piece of cloth to a bloody head. "Or an act of God, more likely. I got bashed in the head. Knocked me senseless."

"Where's Jonathan?" Ziba asked, not sure if he wanted to hear the answer. "Where's the king?"

"Jonathan's dead," Uthai said. "He insisted on holding the line against the chariots. The sky was full of arrows, and the chariots just mowed us down. We didn't stand a chance. He didn't stand a chance."

He struggled to his feet, his body trembling. "Your father and the king were two of the last ones. I remember—before I was knocked out—the king asking his armor-bearer to kill him. The boy refused, so the king," he shook his head, and his voice quavered. "The king fell on his sword." Uthai began to sob.

Ziba stepped over the bodies and came to Uthai, wrapping his arms around him.

"So where's the king's body?" Ziba asked softly. "Where's Jonathan's body?"

Uthai sobbed again. "I don't know."

Ziba looked across the slopes of Mount Gilboa at the pile of bodies, most of them Israelites. Achish had gotten his revenge for Michmash. And Jonathan, the man who had cost Achish that battle, was one of the first to die.

Chapter 18

What Remains

I t was Ziba's first time to deal with loss on a major scale. His mother died when he was only a boy, so he had few memories of her. His father had been his only blood relative, but Jonathan had been the next thing to blood. Ziba shook himself and cried. He *was* blood. He was his brother.

And now Jonathan was gone. His father, Achim, was gone. Even Saul, the king who had reigned over Israel for the past forty years, was gone. Ziba was lost. He had no home, no people, no one to return to. The battle around them was over, and they had lost. And Ziba realized what losing really meant. He hadn't lost before this, and he didn't like the taste of it.

Ziba fell to the ground next to his father and stared down the slope to the valley before him, his eyes barely registering the bodies that blanketed the hillside. Wrecked chariots, dead horses, and thousands of black arrows in bodies and in the ground added to chaos that was overwhelming. After a while, Uthai came and sat down next to Ziba on the ground.

"What do we do now?" Ziba said.

Uthai shrugged. "All of my adult life I've been a soldier in Saul's army. It's all I know." He looked over his shoulder at where Saul's body had been. There he saw only blood and an empty space. "I suppose I can try to find David. Now that David is in charge, he'll be looking for soldiers."

See 1 Samuel 31

Ziba shook his head. "Eshbaal* is still in Gibeah. Some people won't want David as king. They'll try to crown Ish-Bosheth." Ziba paused. "Abner is still around."

"Eshbaal is just a boy," Uthai said.

"He's royal blood," Ziba said. "And in some people's eyes, that's more important than his ability to rule. But my money is on the new guy. If anyone can do a good job of leading, it's David." He turned and looked at Uthai's bloody face. "You sure you don't need some attention?"

Uthai waved his hand. "This isn't anywhere as bad as when I lost the ear. I'll be fine." He stood. "So where are you going?"

Ziba remained seated. "I need to find out what happened to Jonathan and his brothers—and the king," he said. "I owe Jonathan that much."

Uthai squinted into the setting sun in the west. "Funny how the Philistines cleared out so fast. Just goes to show that they were only here to kill Saul." He turned back to Ziba. "I would suspect that they either took the bodies back with them as trophies or put them on display somewhere. But hauling bodies all that way back isn't their style."

Uthai helped Ziba to his feet and then held out his hand and shook Ziba's.

"Stay safe. Go with God," Uthai said.

"You too," Ziba said. "It was a pleasure to serve with you."

"The pleasure was mine." Uthai turned and hobbled down the slope toward the valley, limping as he walked. In a few minutes, Ziba was alone.

Where to start? Ziba thought. Would he have to travel all the way to Philistia? Uthai said that taking the bodies back there was unlikely, so they would probably have left them somewhere for Israel to see the fate of their king and crown prince. Ziba frowned and decided that with no other options available, he would head to the nearest town, a walled city called Beth-shan.

Beth-shan didn't have the best reputation. Whenever Saul was at war, whether it was the Ammonites, the Amalekites, or the Philistines, the people of Beth-shan always seemed to side with whoever was against Israel. Where Jabesh-gilead felt a bond with Saul and his people and

---

* Also called Ish-bosheth.

an obligation that went back more than thirty years, Beth-shan held an unexplainable grudge, probably for the same amount of time.

Ziba walked straight north and then turned east when he got to the road that followed the valley. It was dark by the time he got near the city gates of Beth-shan. And even from a distance, he could see that something was wrong.

When he got closer, he saw two things. First, in the light of torches, he saw that four bloody bodies had been tied to the walls with ropes, hanging next to the entrance so that everyone who entered could see them. Second, the heads of the bodies had been removed. Three were impaled on spikes above the gate. In addition to the missing heads, their armor had been removed. But as Ziba looked closer, he recognized the clothing of Saul and Jonathan. He dropped to his knees as he saw them. It had only been a few hours since the battle, and the Philistines—or the people of Beth-shan—had already insulted the memory of Saul and his sons in a way they couldn't have been insulted while they were alive.

Even as he knelt there in the dust of the road, tears streaming down his face, he heard others arguing with the guards at the gate about the ugly display.

"But the bodies will reek," a woman was saying. "They will attract the crows and the vultures. I know you didn't like the king, but no one should meet a fate like that. No one."

The guard shook his head. "I don't have any say in the matter, woman. Even the city fathers didn't make this decision. The Philistines said the bodies needed to stay until they were nothing but bones. Then we are to take the bones and scatter them over the battlefield and let the dogs eat them. They only saved the head of King Saul to decorate their temple to Dagon. If we don't follow their orders, they'll come back and burn our town to the ground."

Vultures? Dogs? That's not going to happen, Ziba thought. His first impulse was to charge the guards, take them out, and cut the ropes to retrieve the bodies. But he knew that the project would take more than one person. He looked down the road to the east. It had been many years since he'd been here, but he knew that the road east led to Jabesh-gilead. He could find help there.

An hour later, he was at the gates of Jabesh-gilead. A guard was stationed over the walled entrance to the city.

"Who goes there?" the voice asked. "What do you want at this hour?" Ziba noticed that the voice quavered more than a soldier's voice might.

"I'm Ziba, armor-bearer for Jonathan, the crown prince," he said. "I need help from the men of Jabesh-gilead."

He lost sight of the guard as he moved away to talk to someone behind the wall. A few moments later, a woman's voice came down.

"The men of Jabesh-gilead are in short supply these days," the woman said, and Ziba felt that the voice sounded familiar. "They've all gone to fight with Saul against the Philistines. We have no more to offer."

"If you say you have no more to offer, then this isn't the generous city of Jabesh-gilead I remember."

There was a long pause, then the doors opened in front of him. He stepped forward. An old man and a woman stood on the other side, the woman holding a torch.

"Ziba, is that you?" the woman said, and Ziba instantly saw that it was Mara. He rushed forward, then hesitated as he saw her flinch. He smiled thinly and nodded.

"We lost the battle," Ziba said. "Almost everyone is dead."

The old man put his hand to his mouth, and Mara looked as though she would faint but quickly recovered.

"If the battle is over, what do you need from us?" she asked.

"I got to the battlefield too late. Uthai told me that Jonathan, his brothers, and the king were killed." Ziba intentionally left out how the king had died. "But when I got there, their bodies were missing."

"Maybe they weren't killed after all," the old man said.

"They were killed, believe me," Ziba said. "I found their bodies. Missing their heads, and tied to the walls of Beth-Shan."

"That's not right," the old man said.

Ziba shook his head. "No, it's not right. That's why I came here. To find some men to help me get them down."

Mara looked at Ziba, years of missed communication coming through her eyes.

"Like I said, the men are all gone to the battle. All of them. Including my husband and his two oldest sons." Her voice started to choke when she got to the end. "All that's left is a wife and three small sons."

Ziba looked at Mara, torn between relief that he could finally see her after all these years and compassion for a woman who most likely had lost her husband and two sons. Mara saw his face and, as usual, was the one who took action.

"What can we do to help?"

Ziba paused, the wheels turning in his head. Finally, he spoke.

"We need one person to release the ropes, another to load the bodies onto a wagon. The trouble is, the guards are everywhere, and they won't cooperate."

Mara nodded. "Then you need someone to create a diversion," she said. "I have just the boys for the job."

"Boys?" Ziba said.

As he scaled the wall into the city of Beth-shan, Ziba had flashbacks about the cliff climbing they had done at Michmash. He could almost see Jonathan ahead of him on the cliff face, the rocks and dust falling into his eyes and onto his head.

"*Watch it,*" he'd hissed, frustrated with the dirt and rocks and the challenge of climbing in the dark. Now he missed those days, missed Jonathan, and saw this as a small step toward redemption for all the terrible things he'd done since that night. This wall was more sheer, but Ziba had no trouble scaling it. He counted each broken nail, each straining muscle as penance. Before he knew it, he was on the wall.

Two guards were on the wall as well, but their attention was focused toward the front. He had no trouble stepping behind the first guard and wrapping his arm around his throat, cutting off his breathing and causing him to collapse, alive but out of commission for a while. A moment later, he did the same to the second guard.

Then he waved his torch at Mara and the others, who waited in the dark. A moment later, a young woman with three boys walked toward the front gates. The guard stopped them outside the gates. Ziba heard the guard talking to them in hushed tones, but Ziba knew he was telling them they couldn't enter the gates after dark.

"What do you mean we can't enter?" Mara asked. "I have three young boys who need to get home to their beds. What am I supposed to do with them?"

"It's not my concern," Ziba heard the guard say. As if on cue, he heard one of the boys begin to cry, a second begin to argue with his mother and with the guard, and the third let go of his mother's hand and bolt for the gate.

"Jabek!" she shouted after the one who had left. "Come back here!"

The noise and confusion were too much for the guard, and within moments three more guards had come to join them. When they came outside, the oldest boy bolted through the partially open gate. One of the guards ran after him. The other two boys, one crying and another screaming, held the attention of the other guards. Mara chased them through the gate, and the three guards followed her. Ziba smiled to himself; Mara and her sons were doing a spectacular job of diverting their attention.

Ziba turned away from them and paid attention to his task. While they had been taking the guards' attention, the old man from Jabesh-gilead—Ashim was his name, Ziba had learned—had driven a wagon with an ox to a space below the wall. Ziba ran down the top of the wall to the ropes that were tied across to poles on the inside of the wall. One by one, he untied the four ropes and let the bodies drop slowly to the ground. He looked over the edge and saw Ashim below, pulling the bodies into the wagon. Ziba was almost done, but there was one crucial thing left to do.

He ran across the wall to the area just above the gate. There, impaled on stakes, were the heads of Jonathan and his two brothers. The two brothers, Ishvi and Malki-Shua, were easily identifiable. Jonathan's head was bloody and crushed beyond recognition. Saul's head was nowhere to be seen. Ziba paused before them.

"Forgive me, my brother," Ziba said, a choke in his voice. He then drew his sword and hacked each stake in two. He grabbed the heads before they fell to the ground, putting them gingerly into a sack that he carried on his belt. Two minutes later, he was on the ground and running to meet the others on the road to Jabesh-gilead.

The six of them built a large bonfire outside the gate of Jabesh-gilead.

Residents of the town joined them one family at a time, at first surprised that someone would set a bonfire ablaze in the middle of the night. Then the story of the battle and the death of Saul, Jonathan, and his brothers passed through the crowd. As many realized that their husbands and sons wouldn't be returning, they began to cry. The bonfire became a symbol of what they had lost.

"We'll collect the bones, what is left of them, when the fire dies down," Ashim said. "Then we'll bury the bones underneath the tamarisk tree in the center of town. King Saul was always partial to that tree."

Ziba looked at the edge of the fire and saw something glint in the light. Taking a stick, he pulled the object free. He picked it up, not noticing that the object was singeing his hand, and wiped it off.

He looked down at a simple silver ring with a red stone and a hawk etched into the front. Then he turned his hand and looked at his own ring. They were identical. He turned to Ashim and held out Jonathan's ring.

"Make sure this gets buried under that tree as well, will you?" he said, and the old man nodded.

Ziba stood next to Mara, both of them staring into the flames. Without thinking, he reached for her hand. She pulled it away, and Ziba wondered if it was instinctive or intentional. He paused before speaking.

"Your husband," Ziba said. "Was he good to you?"

"*Was*," Mara echoed. "You say that as if you already knew that he was dead." She paused. "What am I saying? Of course he's dead. I know it in my heart." The tears began to flow. Ziba hesitated, not knowing what to do. He finally placed his hand awkwardly on her shoulder as she cried.

"Yes, he was a good man," she said finally through tears. "He loved me, in his own way. And I loved him for taking good care of me and for being a good father." She looked at Ziba, and he saw a faint, familiar light in her eyes. "But it wasn't the same. It'll never be the same."

Ziba nodded awkwardly. "What now?" he asked her.

She shrugged. "He has a brother in Shechem. Elias. He's older, bald, fat. He's not an ideal catch. But he'll support the boys as they grow up.

They can learn a trade. It's something."

Ziba paused again. "Maybe you don't have to leave."

Mara looked at him, then shook her head. "It's too late, Ziba. Too much has happened. We're two different people."

Ziba nodded. "I know that. I missed my chance. But I need somewhere to call home. Everyone I know is gone. Jabesh-gilead is as good a place as any." He looked around him. "I've always liked it here."

"What will you do?" Mara asked. "There's no call for soldiers here."

Ziba looked at her and showed a tired smile. "My father was a blacksmith. There's no reason why I can't be one too. Maybe we can help each other out."

The next six months were happy ones for Mara and Ziba. Neither one brought up their former relationship again. Mara never got word on the fate of her husband and two stepsons, but they never returned. Ziba took on one, then another, of her young sons as apprentices, and in exchange, Mara invited him to dinner once in a while.

Ziba relearned what it was like to work iron and bronze, and his business grew. As he became more successful, he became known in the community. And inevitably there was talk about the widow and the successful, eligible bachelor.

One especially hot day, Ziba took a break from his work over his anvil and the hot forge and walked to the center of town to once again look at the tamarisk tree and contemplate the four men who were buried beneath it. To his surprise, Mara was already there.

"I appreciate your help with my sons," Mara said, still looking at the tree. "They idolize you."

"They're good boys," he said. "They're good apprentices."

He reached over suddenly and grasped Mara by the shoulders, turning her around to face him.

"I know you have other options, Mara," he said. "Any man would be lucky to have a woman like you. You're beautiful, courageous, and smart. But that night, around the fire, you talked about your husband. You said he loved you, after a fashion. And you said you loved him for taking care of you and the boys. But to me, that's not love. I know what love is. Love is that catch in your breath when you see the other person, or even if you're just thinking about her. Love is a racing heart; it's living for the other person. Love is sacrificing your needs for the needs of others. Love is feeling better when you're with someone than when you're alone." He paused and looked at her intently.

"And you deserve someone who loves you."

"And who would that be?" she asked, an edge in her voice.

"You're close enough to touch him, and yet you're blind," Ziba said, realizing the words were familiar.

"Who do you propose I marry? You? Ha! That'll be the day."

Ziba was shocked to hear the words. He stepped back and dropped his hands from her shoulders.

And then he saw the twinkle in her eye and the smile on her lips.

Chapter 19

Just Two Old Men

TWENTY-SIX YEARS LATER

Ziba lay awake on the bed next to Mara, the curtains on the open window moving in the wind. He sensed the hoofbeats long before he heard them. The distant clicking of the horse's hooves on the stone pathway leading through Jabesh-gilead grew louder, and Ziba could make out two, then three, and then four separate horses. The rapid rhythm of the beats told him that someone was in a hurry. And somehow he knew they were coming for him.

Mara began to move under the blanket as the noise grew louder. She tossed as if to get out of bed, but Ziba put a reassuring hand on her.

"Sleep, my wife," he said. "I know what they want. I'll deal with this." As if on command, the sound of the loud hoofbeats ceased. A few seconds later, Ziba could hear a low murmuring of voices and a horse nickering. They were going to come charging into his home any minute, Ziba knew, and he didn't want Mara frightened. He threw on his robe and pushed back the door before they could approach.

Ziba could see it was several hours till dawn. A new moon rose over the field, bleaching all color from the landscape. Four soldiers stood by their horses about fifty feet away, continuing to talk to one another quietly. The town was laid out with small shops on the east end of the street, and his blacksmith pit on the far west end. The soldiers had stopped in the middle of the street, still apparently unsure where they were going.

Ziba closed the door behind him and strode toward the four armored

See 2 Samuel 9

men. They stopped talking and turned to face the old man as he approached them.

"May I help you men find something?" Ziba asked quietly.

"We're looking for Ziba ben-Achim, the blacksmith."

"You found him."

The tallest one, apparently the leader, stepped forward. His face was pinched and sharp, with the characteristics of a hawk, with a hooked nose, receding brown hair, and high cheekbones. Ziba could also see that it had been a long while since the man had smiled or laughed. Like the others, the soldier wore an iron helmet, chest plate, and greaves over leather. The iron had been polished to a high sheen and shone brightly in the moonlight. He stepped forward and reached out to grab Ziba's arm in a viselike grip.

"I am Nim, captain of the guard. You are summoned before the king. Come with us." Ziba's first reaction was to pull away from the grasp of the soldier, but the tone of the man told him that resisting would be unwise. He looked into the expressionless eyes of the young man and then nodded.

"I know you're just doing your duty, fine sir," Ziba said. "And I'm willing to come along with you gladly. Please let go of my arm."

The pinched-faced young man stared at Ziba for a long moment, then nodded, releasing his grip. Another soldier brought a horse forward, and Ziba realized that there had been five horses, not four. *I must be slipping*, he thought. He mounted the brown mare quickly, more quickly than the soldiers had expected an old blacksmith to be able to, and the five of them headed south toward Jerusalem.

They rode quickly through the night, the four soldiers saying nothing, and Ziba lost in thoughts of years past. A lot had happened since he'd last traveled this road on horseback. A blacksmith was not expected to own a horse, much less know how to ride one. And after years of excitement and danger, the simple life of a blacksmith and the love of a wife was all that Ziba wanted.

The miles passed quickly, and soon he could see the lights of Jerusalem on the hilltop in front of them. The horses galloped through the main gate, the soldiers on duty there snapping to attention as the five of them rode into the courtyard, stopping in front of two blazing torches and a large entryway above stone stairs.

The soldier who had identified himself as Nim got off his horse, and the others followed suit. He handed the reins of his horse to one of the others, and Ziba did the same.

"Come with me," he barked at Ziba, then softened as he realized that the old man was no threat. "Come with me, please," he repeated more quietly.

Ziba smiled at him and nodded. Nim led Ziba up the stairway and through the heavy wooden doors into a long passageway that was also lit by torches. The hallway was empty, except for two more soldiers standing at attention at the end of the hall. Once again, their armor shone in the torchlight, and Ziba shook his head.

"Something bothering you?" Nim asked, curious.

"That bright armor may look pretty, but it's very impractical," Ziba said. "The sheen would draw all attention to you on the battlefield."

A line cut across Nim's face, and Ziba realized that he could smile. He shrugged. "It's ceremonial. Made for show. But don't let that fool you. Those men are some of the best soldiers in all of Israel, all battle-tested."

Nim pulled another set of heavy wooden doors open, and the two of them stepped through into what Ziba realized was the throne room. Ziba stared up at the tall ceiling, bronze chandelier with candles in it, and stone floor and pillars. At the far end of the room, the royal throne sat on top of a low, wide platform. To one side of it, something long and flat was on display there. Standing beside it, wrapped in royal robes, a man stood with his back to them.

Nim hesitated and then approached the platform and the man on it. Ziba followed him and stopped with him about twenty feet from the throne. The man on the platform paid no attention to them, apparently lost deep in thought. Eventually, Nim cleared his throat awkwardly, and the man on the platform turned toward them.

"Your Majesty, you asked that Ziba the blacksmith be brought to you," Nim said quietly, dipping his head toward the king. King David's face, showing evidence that he was still lost in thought, nodded. Then, a second later, his expression changed, and the wrinkled brow softened. He looked in the direction of Ziba, and Ziba saw the years fall away. For an instant, Ziba caught a glimpse of the young man who had dazzled thousands and had every young girl in the nation singing about him. Then just as quickly, the innocent youth was gone, replaced by a face filled with worry.

"Leave us," David said to Nim, waving his hand dismissively. "I doubt this man is any risk to us." David stepped forward and peered into Ziba's face. "You're not dangerous, are you, my friend?"

Rather than respond, Ziba bowed low and looked at the floor.

"I'm your servant, Your Majesty," Ziba said.

Nim turned and left, and David stood before Ziba, who remained with his head bowed. Ziba waited for the command for him to rise, but it didn't come. Instead, David turned and started to walk away.

"Come here," he said. "Look at what I have."

Ziba raised his head, then stepped forward onto the platform. David led him to a model of a building that stood supported on a table.

"Do you know what this is?"

"No, Your Majesty."

"This is a model of God's sanctuary. I've designed it for construction here in Jerusalem. I've drawn up all the plans to the last detail. I've gathered the materials from across the known world. I've recruited the best craftsmen from every trade. It will be the finest building in the nation, in the world, worthy to be called God's temple. There's only one problem."

"What's that, Your Majesty?"

"God won't allow me to build it!" As he said the word *build*, King David reached down and turned the table over. The model on top slid to the floor, and the table and model crashed in a heap. King David stared at the pile of wood for a moment before turning to Ziba, a hurt look now in his eyes.

"God has told me that there's blood on my hands." He held his hands out as if looking for the blood. "Because of the hundreds—thousands—of men I've killed over the years, God has told me that another has been chosen to do this task. It would be the crowning achievement of my reign, and *God won't let me do it!*"

Ziba stood still and watched the man pace in agony.

"I . . . I'm not sure why you tell me this, my king," Ziba said. "I'm not a builder, and I definitely have no control over what God allows His anointed king to do. That's between you and God."

"I brought you here because I remember who you are," the king said. His voice sent a chill into Ziba. *He knows.*

"I'm a simple blacksmith, Your Majesty," Ziba said, bowing again.

"Ah, but you weren't always a blacksmith," David said. "There was a time when blacksmiths were outlawed in our country. Then you were something very different—a fighting man. Weren't you?"

Ziba paused, trying to find the correct words that would answer the king truthfully without incriminating himself.

"I . . . I was a servant," Ziba said. "I come from a family of servants."

"We're all servants," David said, staring at the old man. Finally, he nodded.

"I brought you here to ask you a question. The question is this: Why does God choose to exalt one of His people—His *servants*—while others never receive the same recognition? Why does God give one man a special task to do, at the same time taking the task away from another man, just as worthy? Why would He choose me to be king and you a blacksmith?"

Ziba stared at David, open-eyed.

"Because—because He is God," Ziba said finally.

David nodded. "There's another reason."

Ziba continued to stare at the king.

"I'm not sure what Your Majesty wants me to tell you."

"I'm referring to a righteous man whom we both knew and we both loved. I want you to tell me why God chose him to die and me to live. I want to know why you're a servant and I'm a king."

David paced back and forth on the platform.

"Do you remember that day in the field? It was the last day that Jonathan and I ever saw each other. We each made a vow, an oath that we'd take care of each other's family." He paused. "Is there anyone left of Jonathan's kin?"

At first, Ziba was afraid that David had fallen into the habit that most kings practiced, that of killing off any potential rival heir to the throne. But then he realized that David was sincere and there was nothing to fear.

"There is one, Your Majesty," he said. "When Saul and Jonathan were killed, I heard that the palace was abandoned. Everyone in the family was killed in the days to come, including his older son Jethro.

In the rush, a nursemaid dropped his youngest son, Mephibosheth. He lost the use of his legs from that fall. He's still alive, in Lo Debar."

"Does he have a wife? Children?"

Ziba shook his head. "He has a son named Mica."

David stared at him and then shook his head in disbelief. "He's Jonathan's son. I've sworn an oath, and I'll keep it. Here's what I'll do. Listen closely, Ziba."

David called forward his scribe, who began to write as David spoke.

"From this day forward, Mephibosheth, heir of Jonathan, heir of Saul, first king of Israel, will inherit all the lands and properties once belonging to Saul. He'll sit at the table of the king, and come and go from the palace, as he wants. And you," David pointed at Ziba. "You'll be his servant. Will you do these things, Ziba?"

Ziba was surprised that King David gave him a choice.

"Yes, Your Majesty," Ziba said. "I'd be honored to serve the son of Jonathan."

"You and your family will serve the family of Saul. How many sons do you have, Ziba?"

"Fifteen, Your Majesty," Ziba said.

"Fifteen? My, you've been busy all these years," David said, raising an eyebrow. "Making up for lost time?"

"Yes, Your Majesty. God has been kind and given me a loving and wonderful wife."

"Ah yes, Mara. I always thought that she was the better of the two. Michal and I were married for several years, but she never had children. Then she didn't agree on how I served as king. She died about ten years ago. Now she's just a memory." David turned and looked at the model of the sanctuary that lay on the floor, suddenly lost in his thoughts. "Some of us are born to build things, and some of us are born to tear them down."

There was silence as Ziba thought again of Jonathan, and he saw that David was thinking the same thing.

"And some are like a candle that burns brightly and is gone," David added finally. "Go back to your wife and tell her the news."

Ziba nodded, bowed, turned, and went back to Mara.

END